Introduction to Portfolio Rationalization

ISBN-13: 978-1-61580-011-7

ISBN-10: 1-61580-011-5

All questions and comments concerning this publication should be directed to publisher@weatherfordpress.com

Special thanks to Saraa Elhagehammoud for the cover art and much of the artwork throughout the volume. Special thanks to our editors and reviewers, Saraa Elhagehammoud, Lacy Kolo, Mindelin Logar, and Ashley Wright.

Introduction to Portfolio Rationalization

1 Introduction

Portfolio rationalization is the process of analyzing the assets or investments in a portfolio to determine how the investments should be adjusted to better align the portfolio with the strategy of the organization. Rationalization quantifies the business value of each investment in order to create metrics that can be used to compare different investments. The analysis ranks the various assets and identifies opportunities to strengthen the portfolio by adjusting the portfolio components.

Financial v. Non-Financial Portfolios

There are many different types of portfolios. For our purposes, we will categorize portfolios as financial and non-financial. Financial portfolios are investments in stocks, bonds, mutual funds, or other securities. Non-financial portfolios are investments in projects, programs, equipment, etc.

The principal difference between these types of portfolios is the ability to quickly transfer investments between different assets. Financial portfolios typically have the ability to sell one asset and use the cash to purchase another asset. In financial portfolios, the investment has an intrinsic value that may be readily sold. Furthermore, alternative investments are abundantly available, providing a means to easily transfer funding in one asset to a different asset.

Non-financial portfolios typically do not have the ability to quickly transfer between assets. For example, a portfolio of projects has an ongoing financial investment in each project. However, we cannot 'sell' a project and take the funds to start a new project. We either need to see the project through to the end and receive the benefits of the project deliverables, or we can terminate the project to free up funds for other work. That being said we typically cannot recover the sunk costs up to the point of termination.

These differences make analysis of non-financial portfolios different than financial portfolios. Financial portfolio rationalization must be able to quickly react to changing financial circumstances, evaluate an investment, and make a buy/hold/sell decision. The value placed on an asset is usually easy to compute as it is simply the market value of the asset.

In contrast, non-financial portfolio rationalization does not need to react as quickly, but the valuation of the investment is much more difficult. Many projects have an estimated Return-On-Investment (ROI) that can be used to value the investment. Some investments, however, have little or no ROI, but possess a very high business value. For example, a program committed to applying a Government regulation to a business operation may not have a specific ROI, but this program may be extremely valuable to the business in order to assure the business is able to continue operations uninterrupted.

In the following pages, we will focus on non-financial portfolio rationalization. Financial portfolio rationalization has many well developed tools and techniques to measure investment value and risk and make recommendations for the adjustment of assets. Here, we will develop and examine the tools and techniques that may be used in non-financial portfolio rationalization in order to increase the performance of the portfolio.

In discussing financial v. non-financial portfolios, it is important to understand that a financial system (software, processes, etc.) belongs in a non-financial portfolio. Many large organizations have extensive financial systems. These systems, and the projects and processes that support them, are non-financial investments.

Problems in Non-Financial Portfolio Management

The management of non-financial portfolios faces different challenges than their financial counterparts. Investments in non-financial portfolios are typically not liquid, have multiple dimensions to their valuation, and rely heavily on performance forecasts rather than real-time performance.

Portfolio Managers of non-financial portfolios do not have the flexibility to quickly remove a poorly performing asset and replace it with a different investment. This lack of liquidity makes it difficult for the Portfolio Manager to quickly react to changing conditions.

Financial portfolios are typically comprised of liquid assets. There are many standard, well known techniques used in financial portfolio management that rely on the liquidity of the assets in making investment selection. Because the techniques assume investment liquidity, they are not as useful when applied to non-financial portfolios.

In addition, the portfolio investments often have a multi-dimensional nature to their valuation. An investment may be measured in terms of its cost or its return-on-investment. But an investment may also bring regulatory or legal compliance, employee satisfaction, or strategic direction. In order to understand non-financial investments, we must incorporate these other value dimensions into our analysis.

It is essential to account for the multi-dimensional nature of the asset. Simply examining an asset against its return will not provide a true understanding of the value of the investment to the organization. We need to consider the *purpose* of the investment in addition to its cost, return, or other financial factors.

Furthermore, the investments in non-financial portfolios usually rely on forecasts rather than actual results. Most projects are unique. The exact methodology, purpose, personnel, and technology used for a project are unique and different than all other projects in the organization. This makes it difficult to accurately predict how successful the project will be.

Managers typically rely heavily on forecasts when choosing to begin a new project. These forecasts may be quantitatively detailed, estimating the cost and return for the project, or the forecasts may simply be 'I think this is a good direction.' In either case, the selection of the project will rely heavily on forecasts of the benefits the project may bring rather than the actual performance of the project during execution.

These are a few of the common problems faced by managers of non-financial portfolios. These problems lead to questions of how investments should be valued, how investment selection is made, how to compare investments, and how to determine when an investment should be eliminated.

In order to address these problems, we need a formal process for understanding how each of these questions is answered and how we incorporate these answers into a system to manage an investment portfolio. The process should provide a roadmap for the various activities that need to be considered, how they fit together, and what they produce.

Portfolio Rationalization as a Process

This book formalizes the process of portfolio rationalization. We specify the activities involved in portfolio rationalization as a series of processes. Each process has inputs, outputs, and tools and techniques used to execute the process.

We begin in Chapter 2 with some preliminary tools used in portfolio rationalization. These concepts are referred to in later sections, but are not essential for understanding the interactions between the processes themselves. The reader may skip these mathematical foundations and move directly into the rationalization processes.

Chapter 3 presents the main Portfolio Rationalization Process. These processes form the backbone of portfolio rationalization. Each process is described, along with the process inputs, outputs, and tools and techniques used in executing the process.

Chapter 4 presents the portfolio rationalization lifecycle. Portfolio rationalization is an ongoing, continuous endeavor with processes feeding each other both forward and backward along the process flow. This chapter shows how the processes fit together, and how the outputs of one process feed to the inputs of other processes.

Chapters 5, 7, and 9 detail the Investment Model, Portfolio Model, and Rationalization Model. These models are outputs of processes from the Portfolio Rationalization Process provided in Chapter 3. However, these models are crucial elements in the process and are given additional detail. The Investment Model computes the values for each of the investments. The Portfolio Model computes performance metrics and values for the entire portfolio. The Rationalization Model is used to identify investments for rationalization and organizational Best Practices.

Chapter 10 examines methods for introducing the Portfolio Rationalization Process to an organization. Most organizations have some process for rationalization already. This chapter examines where to begin and how to incorporate preexisting ideas into a formal Portfolio Rationalization Process.

Chapter 11 examines some advanced mathematical tools used in portfolio rationalization. This chapter provides a launching point for understanding some of the advanced mathematical ideas that may be employed to perform portfolio rationalization.

Chapter 12 presents a Rationalization Maturity Model. This model evaluates the maturity of an organization's rationalization process. Additionally, the model provides a direction for improving an organization's rationalization process, incorporating automated rationalization tools, and using the rationalization process to improve the Investment, Portfolio, and Rationalization Models.

Portfolio Rationalization Motivation: Cost Savings and Best Practices

The main motivation for employing the Portfolio Rationalization Process is to achieve cost savings by identifying and correcting inefficiencies in the portfolio. The rationalization process achieves cost savings by recommending project/program elimination, consolidation, and identifying redundancies.

Once an investment (project/program) is targeted for rationalization, a Transformation Plan is created detailing how the recommended action is carried out. The Transformation Plan is the final output of the rationalization process incorporating the results from the previous processes together into a single plan for action for modifying the portfolio.

Portfolio Rationalization also identifies investments that are performing well. Examining these investments creates an opportunity to identify the Best Practices in place within the organization.

Well performing investments are carefully examined to identify why they are performing well and identify the fundamental reasons for their success. These Best Practices are documented and the other investments are examined in light of these practices to identify opportunities to apply these practices in other areas. This helps to drive other portfolio investments toward the most successful investments, improving the overall performance of the entire portfolio.

Portfolio Rationalization Motivation: Regulatory Compliance

Another motivation for portfolio rationalization is the regulatory requirements of the Clinger-Cohen Act. This law directs that the Executive branch must administrate IT investments as a portfolio.

Portfolio Rationalization is part of a Congressional mandate from the Clinger-Cohen Act of 1996. This act requires Federal Executive branch Agencies to use portfolio management to handle their IT investments. Although this act is specifically directed toward IT related investments, Portfolio Rationalization may be effectively used in non-IT environments as well.

In the following sections we discuss the Clinger-Cohen Act and the agency response to this regulatory requirement. Essentially, Executive branch Departments issue their own interpretation of how this Act impacts their IT investments. Moreover, individual Agencies within the Departments interpret these Department level specifications.

The mandate begins with the Clinger-Cohen Act. This Act is interpreted by the Office of Management and Budget (OMB) and passed down to the Departments. The Departments then issue requirements to their Agencies. The Agencies in turn issue guidelines on how to comply with these regulations within the Agency. The sections below provide some details on the various interpretations of the Clinger-Cohen Act.

Clinger-Cohen Act of 1996

The Clinger-Cohen Act of 1996[1] (Act) instructs the Director of the Office of Management and Budget (Director) to promote improvements in the use of information technology by the Federal Government.[2] Specifically, this Act is directed toward improvements in the productivity, efficiency, and effectiveness of Federal programs. [3] The Act instructs the Director to develop a process for analyzing, tracking, and evaluating the risks and

---

[1] (National Defense Authorization Act of 1996) § E – Information Technology Management Reform Act of 1996.
[2] (Information Technology Reform Act of 1996) (Information Technology Reform Act of 1996) § 5112b.
[3] *Id.*

results of all major capital investments made by an Executive agency of information systems. [4]

In execution of these responsibilities, the head of each Executive agency implements a process for reviewing Information Technology investments, including maximizing their value and managing risks. [5] The Act requires that this process address the following information technology investment concerns: [6]

1. **Selection**[7] – A process for the selection, management, and evaluation of information technology investments.
2. **Integration**[8] – A method to integrate the investment decision with budget, financial, and program management decisions.
3. **Criteria**[9] – State specific criteria applied when considering whether to undertake a particular information technology investment. The criteria must be expressed quantitatively and address net and risk-adjusted return on investment as well as comparing and prioritizing alternative information technology investments.
4. **Shared Investment Identification**[10] – A process for identifying information system investments that may result in benefits if shared between Federal agencies, State, or local governments.
5. **Proposed Investment Benefits**[11] - A process for quantifiably measuring the benefits and risks of a proposed investment.
6. **Progress Measurements**[12] – A process for senior leaders to obtain pertinent information for an investment, including progress, milestones, cost, capability, timeliness, and quality.

OMB – Management of Federal Information Resources A-130

Implementing the Clinger-Cohen Act, the Director of the Office of Management and Budget issued OMB Circular A-130. [13] This circular implemented the requirements of the Clinger-Cohen Act by providing a

---

[4] *Id.* at § 5112c.
[5] *Id.* at § 5122a.
[6] *Id.* at § 5122b.
[7] *Id.* at § 5122b(1).
[8] *Id.* at § 5122b(2).
[9] *Id.* at § 5122b(3).
[10] *Id.* at § 5122b(4).
[11] *Id.* at § 5122b(5).
[12] *Id.* at § 5122b(6).
[13] (Office of Management and Budget Circular A-130)

specific policy for implementation by the heads of Government agencies. The policy specifies the information management policy and the process for implementing the policy.

Information Management Policy

The information management policy addresses nine areas of information management. A brief description of each of these areas is provided below.[14]

1. **Information Management Planning**[15] – Agencies must plan for managing information in an integrated manner throughout the program lifecycle. This includes anticipating the effects of decisions on other stages of the lifecycle, effects on the public, effects on State and Local government, identifying potential for interagency cooperation, information security, privacy considerations, information accessibility, and record retention.

2. **Information Collection**[16] – Agencies are only allowed to create information necessary for the proper performance of agency functions and which has practical utility.

3. **Electronic Information Collection**[17] – In compliance with the Government Paperwork Elimination Act, Executive agencies are required to provide the option of electronic submission and disclosure of information when applicable. Moreover, Executive agencies are directed to accept electronic signatures when practicable.

4. **Records Management**[18] – Executive agencies must ensure that their records provide adequate documentation of agency activities and ensure the ability to access records regardless of form or medium.

5. **Public Disclosure**[19] – The policy specifies several aspects of public disclosure of information balancing the requirements of the Freedom of Information Act and the Privacy Act.

6. **Information Dissemination Management Systems**[20] – Agencies must maintain and implement a management system for all

---

[14] *Id.* at § 8a.
[15] *Id.* at § 8a(1).
[16] *Id.* at § 8 a(2).
[17] *Id.* at § 8 a(3).
[18] *Id.* at § 8 a(4).
[19] *Id.* at § 8 a(5).

information dissemination products meeting certain minimum criteria.

7. **Avoid Restrictive Practices**[21] – Agencies must avoid establishing policies that interfere with the availability of information dissemination products on a timely and equitable basis. This includes the charging of fees or royalties for use of federal dissemination products by the public. However, users may be charged at a level sufficient to recover the cost of dissemination.

8. **Electronic Dissemination**[22] – Agencies are instructed to use electronic formats when appropriate and within budgetary constraints. The policy sets forth guidelines to determine when electronic dissemination is appropriate.

9. **Information Safeguards**[23] – Agencies are directed to ensure that their information is protected in proportion to the risk and magnitude of harm that would result from compromise. Moreover, agencies must limit the collection of information which identifies individuals to that necessary for performance of agency operations. Finally, agencies must provide individuals access to personal information retained by the agency in compliance with the Privacy Act.

Information System and Information Technology Management

This section of the policy addresses information system management, interprets the Clinger-Cohen Act, and specifies policy for the management of information systems. Specifically, policy is provided for governing capital planning, selection, control, and evaluation. In addition, direction is provided for establishing enterprise architecture, standards, and information security concerns.[24]

1. **Capital Planning**[25]– Agencies must establish and maintain a capital planning and investment control process linking mission needs, information, and technology in an efficient manner. The process has three components: selection, control, and evaluation. In addition, two distinct investment plans are identified.

---

[20] *Id.* at § 8 a(6).
[21] *Id.* at § 8 a(7).
[22] *Id.* at § 8 a(8).
[23] *Id.* at § 8a(9).
[24] *Id.* at § 8b.
[25] *Id.* at § 8ab(1).

a. Plans[26]

    i. *Information Resource Management (IRM) Strategic Plan* - This plan is strategic in nature and addresses all information resource management of the agency. The plan includes a description of how information resource management activities help accomplish agency missions, and ensure integration with organizational planning, budget, procurement, financial management, human resources, and program decisions.

    ii. *Information Technology Capital Plan* – This plan is operational in nature and addresses the goals and missions identified in the IRM Strategic Plan. This living document is updated twice each year and is divided into four components that address a variety of regulatory concerns for the agency.

b. Investment Selection[27] – The selection process requires agencies to review thirteen different information related items:

    i. *Investment Evaluation* – Each investment must be evaluated to determine whether the investment will support core mission functions.

    ii. *Development of New Systems* – A new information system may only be developed when there is no alternative government or commercial system that meets the agency needs.

    iii. *Support Efficiencies* – Agencies must support processes that simplify processes, reduce costs, improve efficiencies, and maximize use of commercial off-the-shelf (COTS) technologies.

    iv. *Risk Reduction* – Risk is reduced by isolating and testing custom components.

    v. *Demonstrate ROI* – Information technology investment selection should consider the return-on-investment (ROI) and the selected technology should be projected to have a higher ROI than other potential solutions.

---

[26] *Id.*

[27] *Id.* at § 8b(1)(b).

vi. *Benefit-Cost Analysis* – Agencies must prepare and update a benefit-cost analysis for each information system throughout its life cycle.

vii. *Information Technology Portfolio* – Agencies must maintain a portfolio of major information systems that monitor investments and prevent redundancy of existing or shared IT capabilities.

viii. *Compliance with Federal Enterprise Architectures* – Agencies must ensure consistency with Federal Enterprise Architectures by demonstrating consistency through compliance with agency business requirements and standards.

ix. *Information Technology Improvements* – Agencies must ensure improvements to information systems do not unnecessarily duplicate IT capabilities.

x. *Maximize Useful Information* – A selected system must maximize the usefulness of information, minimize the burden on the public, and preserve the confidentiality of information throughout the life cycle of the information.

xi. *Oversight* – Agencies must establish oversight mechanisms to evaluate and ensure data security, interoperability, and availability.

xii. *Not Unnecessarily Restrictive* – Agencies must ensure that Selected Systems do not unnecessarily restrict the prerogatives of State, Local, and Tribal governments.

xiii. *Accessibility* – Selected Systems must facilitate the accessibility requirements of the Rehabilitation Act of 1973.

c. Investment Control[28] – Agencies are instructed to institute performance measurements to monitor and control investment performance in comparison with actual results. These oversight mechanisms track programs to ensure milestones are met and risks are minimized.

i. *Performance Measures* – Agencies must institute performance measures that monitor actual performance compared to expected results.

---

[28] *Id.* at § 8b(1)(c).

ii. *Periodic Review* – Agencies are required to establish an oversight mechanism to perform periodic reviews of information systems to access how requirements have changed and if the systems fulfill the current and anticipated requirements.

iii. *Progress* – Information systems must progress in a timely manner according to an agreed upon set of milestones.

iv. *Risk Mitigation Strategy* – Agencies must prepare a risk mitigation strategy that identifies and mitigates risk associated with each information system.

v. *Financial System Conformance* – Financial systems must be maintained in conformance with OMB Circular A-127 "Financial Management Systems."

vi. *Enterprise Architecture* – Agency Enterprise Architecture procedures must be followed in accordance with EA milestones.

d. <u>Investment Evaluation</u>[29] - Agencies must routinely evaluate information systems to validate benefits, ROI, and maintenance of Enterprise Architecture information.

i. *Post-Implementation Reviews* – Agencies must conduct post-implementation reviews of information systems and management processes to validate estimated benefits and costs.

ii. *ROI* – Information systems must be evaluated to ensure positive ROI. Moreover, these systems are evaluated to determine whether continuation, modification, or termination is warranted.

iii. *Lessons Learned* – Information system lessons learned must be documented based on the post-implementation reviews.

iv. *Reassessment* – Information systems must be reassessed in terms of their business case, technical compliance, and compliance against the Enterprise Architecture.

v. *Capital Planning Updates* – Agencies must update the Enterprise Architecture, and IT capital planning processes are needed.

---

[29] *Id.* at § 8b(1)(d)

2. **Enterprise Architecture**[30] - Agencies are required to document and submit Enterprise Architecture plans to OMB. This section defines what is required in these submissions.

   a. Enterprise Architecture Definition – Enterprise Architecture is defined as the explicit description and documentation of the current and desired relationships among business and management processes and information technology.

   b. Enterprise Architecture Framework – Agencies are required to create an Enterprise Architecture Framework documenting linkages between mission needs, information content, and information technology.

   c. Technical Reference Model – The Technical Reference Model identifies and describes the information services used throughout the agency.

   d. Standards Profile – The Standards Profile defines the IT standards that support the Technical Reference Model. This includes a Security Standards profile that specifies security services supplied to Enterprise Architecture.

3. **Information System Security**[31] - Agencies are directed to incorporate security measures into the architecture of their information systems.

   a. Prioritization – Agencies must prioritize key systems and apply OMB policies to achieve adequate security commensurate with the level of risk and magnitude of harm.

   b. Explicit – The role of security of information systems must be made explicit.

   c. Funding – OMB will only consider funding systems that meet these requirements.

4. **Acquisition**[32] - Agencies must acquire information technology by utilizing competitive processes designed to reduce risk.

   a. Competition – Procurement must take place with adequate competition and proper allocation of risk between the Government and contractor to maximize ROI.

   b. Segmentation – Agencies must structure major information systems into segments with a narrow scope and brief duration

---

[30] *Id.* at § 8 b(2).

[31] *Id.* at § 8 b(3).

[32] *Id.* at § 8 b(4).

in order to reduce risk, promote flexibility and interoperability, and match mission needs with technology and market conditions.

c. Commercial Products – Agencies must acquire commercial off-the-shelf products unless the cost effectiveness of developing custom software is clear.

d. Accessibility – Agencies must ensure compliance of acquired technologies pursuant to the Rehabilitation Act of 1973.

DODI 8115.02

In support of the Clinger-Cohen Act of 1996 and OMB A-130, the Department of Defense issued Instruction 8115.02. [33] This instruction provides interpretation of the Director's process for information technology portfolio management. The instruction specifically identifies four integrated activities for portfolio management: analysis, selection, control, and evaluation. [34] The process is defined as an iterative process with feedback incorporated to guide future decisions. [35]

1. **Analysis** – Analysis establishes performance goals, identifies gaps and opportunities, provides for continuous improvement, and explores functional and technical options.

2. **Selection** – Selection identifies the best mix of investments from the resources available. Selection decisions are made using integrated architectures, transition plans, technical criteria, and programmatic trade-offs to satisfy performance measures and achieve desired outcomes.

3. **Control** – Control focuses on acquiring the selected capabilities for the portfolio. Control consists of acquisition and oversight at the portfolio level complementing traditional single-platform acquisition.

4. **Evaluation** – Evaluation measures and assesses the outcomes of portfolio investments to determine whether expected benefits are achieved. These results feed back into the previous activities in an iterative process.

5. **Enabler for Information Sharing** – Information technology portfolio management is a key enabler of information sharing across components and communities of interest.

---

[33] (Department of Defense Instruction 8115.02, 2003)
[34] *Id.* at § 6.1.3.
[35] *Id.*

6. **Flexible Process** – Information technology portfolio management is an ongoing, collaborative, and flexible process.

Army Information Technology Portfolio Management Guidelines

Furthermore, the Army has released additional guidance for interpretation of the Department of Defense instructions.[36] This guidance defines evolving processes to ensure information technology investments accomplish the following: [37]

1. **Alignment** – Investments should be aligned to support current operations and transformation.
2. **Warfighter Support** – Investments should provide measurable support to the Warfighter.
3. **Strategic Goals** – Investments should be aligned with the strategic goals and objectives of the Army.
4. **Interoperability** – Investments should ensure interoperability, integration, and configuration to support the Enterprise Architecture.

Information technology portfolio management processes focus on optimizing the capabilities of the Army Enterprise. They are designed to provide the Warfighter the most effective support possible. Specifically, these processes are comprised of the following:[38]

1. **Investment Oversight** – The process facilitates the management and oversight of potential and currently funded investments.
2. **Encourage Architectures** – The process encourages the use of Mission Areas/Domain architecture products to support investment decisions.
3. **Facilitate Existing Processes** – The process also facilitates existing decision processes.
4. **Enterprise-Wide IT Management** – The process allows enterprise-wide participation in the management of IT investments based on objective and measureable criteria.

The information technology process for the Army is defined as a six step process. These steps incorporate the previous directives mentioned in this

---

[36] (Army Information Technology Portfolio Management Guidance, 2008)
[37] *Id.* at Chapter 1 § b.
[38] *Id.* at Chapter 1 § c.

section. They represent a series of the continuous phases used to manage portfolios. [39]

1. **Binning** – Binning is the activity of assigning capabilities/investments to the governing Army IT Mission Areas/Domains.

2. **Criteria Determination** – This is the activity that defines the portfolio goals, assessment metrics, and risk assessment criteria used to analyze the investments. Criteria Determination is typically covered as part of the Analyze activity that follows.

3. **Analyze** – Analyze builds on Requirements Analysis for new and existing IT systems. This activity links portfolio objectives to Enterprise vision, mission, goals, objectives, and priorities. The Analyze phase develops quantifiable outcome-based performance measures, identifies capability gaps, opportunities, redundancies, provides for process improvement, and determines the strategic direction of selected Mission Areas.

4. **Select** – The Select phase identifies and selects the optimal set of prioritized investments to strengthen and achieve capability goals for the portfolio.

5. **Control** – The Control activity ensures the portfolio and investments comprising the portfolio are managed and monitored with quantifiable outcome-based performance measures.

6. **Evaluate** – The Evaluate phase measures the actual contributions of investments within the portfolio. Investments are evaluated against performance measures to determine whether to recommend continuation, modification, or termination of individual investments within the portfolio.

---

[39] *Id.* at Chapter 2 § b.

2 Preliminary Concepts

Fundamentally, portfolio rationalization is the process of eliminating wasteful spending by analyzing the investment properties and restructuring the portfolio to better align with the organizational strategy. The Portfolio Rationalization Process described here details individual processes that may be used to perform portfolio rationalization.

Essentially, portfolio rationalization examines a group of investments by defining a business value that allows comparison of investments. The business value is then used to determine the performance of the investments as well as the portfolio. In addition, the requirements of the investments are analyzed to identify how each investment fits into the portfolio and aligns with the organizational strategy. Business value and Requirements Analysis are used to determine how the portfolio may be restructured to achieve better performance.

However, it should be noted that the Portfolio Rationalization Process should be tailored to an individual organization. It is not necessary to use every process described here, nor are these processes considered an exhaustive list. Rather, the processes described here should be interpreted to demonstrate some of the Best Practices used to implement portfolio rationalization.

This section describes some of the details behind the concepts discussed later in the book. Although this text is not intended to show the details of applying the processes to a particular rationalization effort, some of the concepts discussed may be unfamiliar, and this section provides a basis for some fundamental concepts. Later sections discuss several advanced concepts that may be used to assist in the Portfolio Rationalization Process.

Portfolio

A portfolio is a collection of investments grouped together to achieve a collective purpose. The purpose does not need to have a functional outcome, and the investments may be grouped together even though they are otherwise unrelated.

A portfolio is composed of investments, but the investments do not need to be financial investments. A portfolio may be made up of financial instruments (stocks, bonds, etc.), non-financial investments (projects, programs, etc.), or a combination of the two. By managing the group of investments as a single portfolio, we focus attention on the overall performance of the group rather than the individual performance of a single asset. The terms 'asset' and 'investment' are used interchangeably.

Portfolio rationalization as described here is concerned primarily with non-financial portfolios. Non-financial portfolios are particularly challenging because they often do not have a single, easily quantifiable value that can be used to measure performance. Without such a value, it is difficult to measure the performance of an investment or to make relative comparisons between investments.

Business Value

Value Concept
Business value is used to define a quantifiable, comparable metric unit and measure that helps analyze the investments. Business value is not necessarily measured in dollars. This value may measure employee satisfaction, regulatory compliance, or some other non-financial quantity.

Business Value is a quantification of the value an investment brings to an organization. In financial portfolios, the business value would typically be the market value of the asset. However, in a non-financial portfolio, assigning a value to an investment can be quite complicated.

An organization may have multiple concepts of value that can be assigned to a single investment. For example, a corporate day-care program may have an annual budget of $250K and provide no direct revenue, but it prevents up to $5M in lost employee time. In one sense, this program looses $250K annually. In another sense, the program has a net gain of $4.75M.

Additionally, employees may see this as a significant benefit, and we may assign a value to the day-care program based on the happiness it brings the staff. This value assignment likely will not be in monetary terms, and computing the value is not something that can be done by simply applying a formula to the program spending. Valuations such as these would typically be made by submitting anonymous questionnaires to the employees allowing them to rate programs on a scale from 1-5 or 1-10. The results of these questionnaires can be averaged to find a business value, and the results of one program may be compared with others.

From this example we see that there are three different values that may be applied to this program. Two are measured in monetary terms: cost ($250K) and return ($4.75M). However, there is another value measured in employee satisfaction.

Dimensions and Units

The dimension of a measurement is the physical or logical character of the measurement. Length and time are two fundamental physical dimensions. Units are the particular scale used in measuring a dimension. Length may be measured in units of feet or meters; time is measured in units of seconds.

It is essential to track the units with the values. The simple value of 250,000 has different meaning when the unit is dollars as opposed to chickens. Often values are reported without units. This is only appropriate if the value does not have an underlying unit. However, when there is a unit, it should always be reported with the value.

Comparing Values

We can compare different measurements made in the same units. In the previous example, we can compare the cost and return. These values have a relative meaning and it makes sense to say that the return is nineteen times larger than the cost. We can also compare values made in the same units between investments. Thus, we can compare the cost of the day-care program with the cost of a recycling program. It makes sense to say that the return of the day-care program is greater than the cost.

However, we cannot compare values measured in different units. We cannot compare a $250K cost with an employee satisfaction of 7.9. These values have different units and measurements with different units cannot be directly compared. Thus, it is nonsense to say that the cost of the day-care program is greater than the employee satisfaction.

Combining Values – Derived Units

We can create new units by combining fundamental units. For example, we can create a velocity unit by dividing a length by a time. If I travel 50 miles over 2 hours, my average velocity is 25 miles per hour. Although the derived unit is created by combining fundamental units, the derived unit is still not comparable with the fundamental units. There is no sense in saying that 25 miles per hour is greater than 50 miles.

However, if we have two measurements with the same derived units, we may be able to compare them. If my average velocity is 25 miles per hour and your average velocity is 30 miles per hour, then your average velocity is greater than mine.

This may be a useful method to compare some investments. Using the example above, we can say that the cost per satisfaction of the investment is $250K / 7.9 = $31,646 per satisfaction. We can compare this ratio to the cost per satisfaction of other programs.

We cannot compare two measurements simply because they have the same units. Suppose we have two investments, and we divide the cost of one investment by the satisfaction of the other. The result is measured in dollars per satisfaction, but this is not comparable to the cost per satisfaction measurements above. There is a fundamental difference between the concepts of dividing the cost of an asset by its own satisfaction as opposed to the cost of an asset divided by a different asset's satisfaction. These measurements are simply not comparable, even though they have the same units.

This is somewhat similar to the physical concepts of torque and energy. Both are measured in fundamental units as $kg\frac{m^2}{s^2}$, but they measure different physical properties. Because they have different physical meanings, torque and energy are not comparable, even though they have the same fundamental units.

Risk

Risk in this context is a measure of uncertainty in a value. Risk may be characterized in terms of probability, vulnerability, and impact. These characterizations are a means to formulating a quantitative value for the uncertainty in some value.

A measured value is a particular observation of the value at some instant in time. The measurement is never exact and is always associated with some degree of error. Suppose we have a variable x and measure its value. The measurement may be imagined as having some expected value associated with some error. Designate $\langle x \rangle$ as the expected value and δ_x as the error. A given measurement may be expressed as

$$x = \langle x \rangle + \delta_x \qquad \text{2-1}$$

In this expression, x is the value we measure, $\langle x \rangle$ is what we would get if we repeatedly measured x and averaged the results, and δ_x is the error we associate with any given measurement.

A single measurement of x tells us very little. We have one measurement, but we don't know the average measurement $\langle x \rangle$ or the error δ_x. The error is particularly important in order for us to understand how good the measurement is. A measurement of 5 ± 0.01 is much different than 5 ± 50. Knowing the error helps us to understand how valuable the measurement is.

Before we move on to discuss how we can determine the error, it is important to note a few facts about the expectation$\langle \ \rangle$. In the formulae below, x is a random variable (what we are measuring) and c is an ordinary number.

$$\langle c \rangle = c$$
$$\langle x \rangle = \bar{x}$$
$$\langle cx \rangle = c\langle x \rangle \qquad \text{2-2}$$
$$\langle x + y \rangle = \langle x \rangle + \langle y \rangle$$
$$\langle x + c \rangle = \langle x \rangle + \langle c \rangle = \langle x \rangle + c$$

Mean-Squared Error

The measurement of x is easy enough for us to find; we simply measure its value. However, determining the error is more difficult. Symbolically, we can rewrite the equation 2-1 as

$$\delta_x = x - \langle x \rangle \qquad \text{2-3}$$

To find an expression for the error, we square both sides and take the expectation

$$\langle (\delta_x)^2 \rangle = \langle (x - \langle x \rangle)^2 \rangle \qquad \text{2-4}$$

$$\langle \delta_x^2 \rangle = \langle (x - \langle x \rangle)^2 \rangle. \qquad \text{2-5}$$

Based on this, we can define

$$u_x = \sqrt{\langle (x - \langle x \rangle)^2 \rangle} \qquad \text{2-6}$$

as the uncertainty in the value of the measurement. Alternatively, this expression is also the expression for the standard deviation of a sample

$$\sigma_x = \sqrt{\langle (x - \langle x \rangle)^2 \rangle}. \qquad \text{2-7}$$

Alternatively, σ_x^2 is called the variance of x.

Normal Distribution

The normal distribution is commonly used to describe data that is clustered about an average. The idea underlying the use of the normal distribution is that we cannot know exactly what the value of any given investment is. We can estimate the value through a variety of means, but we cannot know the true value.

For example, assume we have a set of n investments in a portfolio where the value of the investments is V_n and the uncertainty is ΔV_n. V_n is the measured or estimated value of the nth investment. The true value of the investment lies on a normal distribution with mean $\mu = V_n$ and standard deviation $\sigma = \Delta V_n$.

This may be because we simply don't have exact measurements of the investment value, or it may be that the investment value changes over time and we cannot know the precise value at any moment. In any case, we estimate the investment value and use this as V_n. However, we must understand that anytime we make such an estimate, there is some inherent uncertainty in the estimate. The uncertainty is the ΔV_n we associate with the investment value.

Uncertainty exists even when we carefully measure the investment value. For example, we may measure the value of a project using detailed earned value management. Earned value metrics such as percent complete, cost, and other factors vary over time. This fluctuation causes some uncertainty in the true value of the investment.

Mathematically, the probability density for the normal distribution is given by

$$N(x) = \frac{1}{\sigma\sqrt{2\pi}} e^{-\frac{1}{2}\left(\frac{x-\mu}{\sigma}\right)^2}$$

2-8

where μ is the mean and σ is the standard deviation.

Probability Density Function

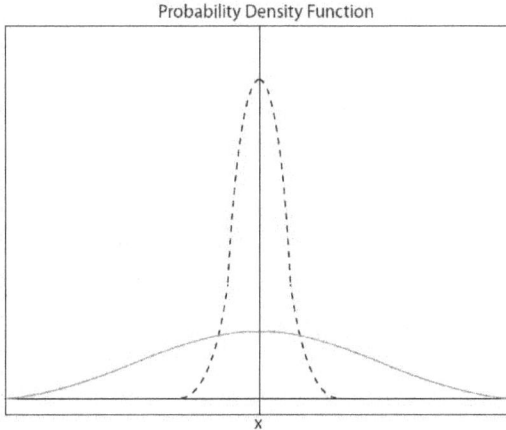

x

Figure 1: Normal Distribution

It should be noted that another probability distribution may be used instead of the normal distribution. Another probability distribution should only be substituted if there is compelling reason to believe that the investment obeys some other distribution. Often, measurements of this type fall on a normal distribution.

Combining Uncertainties

Different sources of risk may lead to different uncertainties that are placed on the same value. This leads to expressions for the measurement such as

$$x = \langle x \rangle + \delta_1 + \delta_2$$

2-9

Substituting this into 2-7,

$$\sigma_x{}^2 = \langle (x - \langle x \rangle)^2 \rangle \qquad \text{2-10}$$

$$= \langle (\delta_1 + \delta_2)^2 \rangle \qquad \text{2-11}$$

$$= \langle \delta_1{}^2 \rangle + \langle \delta_2{}^2 \rangle + 2\langle \delta_1 \delta_2 \rangle. \qquad \text{2-12}$$

Similar to 2-6, we define the uncertainty as

$$u_x{}^2 = u_1{}^2 + u_2{}^2 + 2\langle \delta_1 \delta_2 \rangle. \qquad \text{2-13}$$

The third term is called the covariance of δ_1 and δ_2, (because $\langle \delta_1 \rangle = \langle \delta_2 \rangle = 0$)

$$\sigma^2_{x,y} = \langle xy \rangle - \langle x \rangle \langle y \rangle. \qquad \text{2-14}$$

We can also define the correlation coefficient as

$$\rho_{x,y} = \frac{\sigma^2_{x,y}}{\sigma_x \sigma_y}. \qquad \text{2-15}$$

Writing the uncertainty in terms of these expressions,

$$u_x = \sqrt{u_1{}^2 + u_2{}^2 + 2\rho_{x,y} u_1 u_2}. \qquad \text{2-16}$$

If the sources of error, δ_1 and δ_2, are statistically independent of each other, then their correlation coefficient is zero. In this case the uncertainty reduces to

$$u_x = \sqrt{u_1{}^2 + u_2{}^2}. \qquad \text{2-17}$$

which is just the square root of the sum of the squares of the errors.

Propagation of Errors

We often run across cases where we want to combine measurements as a function. For example, we may want to examine the ratio of two measurements $z = x/y$. We measure x and y and have some associated uncertainties δ_x and δ_y. We need to find the uncertainty to associate with z.

Generally, we set

$$z = f(x, y). \qquad \text{2-18}$$

The error in the measurement of z is determined by applying the total derivative of the expression for z

$$\delta_z = \left(\frac{\partial f}{\partial x}\right) \delta_x + \left(\frac{\partial f}{\partial y}\right) \delta_y. \qquad \text{2-19}$$

Substituting these into 2-16,

$$u_z{}^2 = \left(\frac{\partial f}{\partial x}\right)^2 u_x{}^2 + \left(\frac{\partial f}{\partial y}\right)^2 u_y{}^2 + 2\left(\frac{\partial f}{\partial x}\right)\left(\frac{\partial f}{\partial y}\right)\rho_{x,y}u_xu_y. \qquad \text{2-20}$$

If the measurements of x and y are independent then $\rho_{x,y} = 0$ and we have

$$u_z = \sqrt{\left(\frac{\partial f}{\partial x}\right)^2 u_x{}^2 + \left(\frac{\partial f}{\partial y}\right)^2 u_y{}^2}. \qquad \text{2-21}$$

This is the formula for the propagation of errors.

It is useful to note a few standard error propagation expressions that occur frequently.

Expression	Error Propagation	
$f(x, y) = x + y$	$u_f{}^2 = (1)^2 u_x{}^2 + (1)^2 u_y{}^2 = u_x{}^2 + u_y{}^2$	2-22
$f(x, y) = x - y$	$u_f{}^2 = (1)^2 u_x{}^2 + (-1)^2 u_y{}^2 = u_x{}^2 + u_y{}^2$	2-23
$f(x, y) = xy$	$u_f{}^2 = (y)^2 u_x{}^2 + (x)^2 u_y{}^2 = y^2 u_x{}^2 + x^2 u_y{}^2$	2-24
$f(x, y) = \dfrac{x}{y}$	$u_f{}^2 = \left(\dfrac{1}{y}\right)^2 u_x{}^2 + \left(-\dfrac{x}{y^2}\right)^2 u_y{}^2$ $= \dfrac{y^2 u_x{}^2 + x^2 u_y{}^2}{y^4}$	2-25

Equation 2-22 is of particular note as this expression occurs very frequently. For example, if we know that the value of asset A is $100 ± $10, and the value of asset B is $400 ± $20, the value of the sum of the two is $z = \$100 + \$400 = \$500$. The value of the uncertainty is $u_z = \sqrt{10^2 + 20^2} = \sqrt{500} \approx \$22.4$. Thus, the measurement is $z = \$500 ± \$22.4$.

Often, people add the errors together to get $z = \$500 ± \$30$. This is incorrect. The error propagation formula should be used to properly determine the error from the function.

In fact, one easy way to see that directly adding the errors is incorrect is to look at a subtraction. For example, $x = \$400 ± \$10$, $y = \$100 ± \$10$, with $z = x - y$ evaluates to $z = \$400 - \$100 = \$300$ with $u_z = \sqrt{10^2 + 10^2} = \sqrt{200} \approx \$14$ for the value $z = \$300 ± \$14$. If we were to directly add the uncertainties we would have $z = \$300 ± \$0$!

Probability
Understanding probability is fundamental to the proper application of the principles of risk. A complete treatment of probability is beyond the scope of this book, but the following sections provide some of the key probability

aspects that may be useful in portfolio rationalization. The reader is referred to the references for a more thorough discussion of these and other probability topics.

Expectation[40]

The expectation of a random variable ξ from a probability density $f_X(x)$ is defined as

$$E(\xi) = \langle \xi \rangle = \int_{-\infty}^{\infty} \xi f_X(x) dx \qquad \text{2-26}$$

Conditional Expectation[41]

The conditional expectation of a random variable ξ given an event B such that $P(B) \neq 0$ is given by

$$E(\xi|B) = \frac{1}{P(B)} \int_{B} \xi dP \qquad \text{2-27}$$

Conditional Probability[42]

When we have two events, we may want to know what the probability is of one event occurring given that another event has occurred. This can be particularly useful in Risk Analysis: What is the probability that the data center will shut down given that we have lost power to the main breaker?

This conditional probability is given by

$$P(A|B) = \frac{P(A \cap B)}{P(B)} \qquad \text{2-28}$$

where $P(B)$ is the probability that event B occurs, $P(A \cap B)$ is the probability that both event A and event B occurs, and $P(A|B)$ is the probability that event B occurs given event A has occurred.

Bayes' Theorem

Conditional probability of A given B may be written in terms of the probability of A, B, and the probability of B given A as

$$P(A|B) = \frac{P(B|A)P(A)}{P(B)} \qquad \text{2-29}$$

Bayes' Theorem is the basis of Bayesian statistics.

---

[40] (Brzezniak, 2000)p. 6 Definition 1.9
[41] (Brzezniak, 2000) p. 17 Definition 2.1
[42] (Grigoriu, 2002) p. 16

Joint Probability

The joint probability of A and B may be written in terms of the probability of A given B as

$$P(A, B) = P(A|B)P(B)$$ (2-30)

Independence[43]

Two variables are independent if

$$P(A \cap B) = P(A)P(B)$$ (2-31)

Autocorrelation Function[44]

Let $X(t)$ be a random process. The autocorrelation function $R_X(\tau)$ is

$$R_X(\tau) = \lim_{T \to \infty} \frac{1}{T} \int_{-T/2}^{T/2} X(t)X(t + \tau)dt$$ (2-32)

Crosscorrelation Function[45]

Let $X(t)$ and $Y(t)$ be random processes. The crosscorrelation function $R_{XY}(\tau)$ is

$$R_{XY}(\tau) = \lim_{T \to \infty} \frac{1}{T} \int_{-T/2}^{T/2} X(t)Y(t + \tau)dt$$ (2-33)

Conditional Probability Density[46]

Let $f_{XY}(x, y)$ be be a probability density and $f_X(x)$ the corresponding marginal density. The conditional probability density is

$$f_{Y|X}(y|x) = \frac{f_{XY}(x, y)}{f_X(x)}$$ (2-34)

Independence and Joint Density[47]

Let $f_{XY}(x, y)$ be a joint probability density. X and Y are independent if the joint distribution can be written as the product over the marginal distributions.

---

[43] (Rosenthal, 2008) p. 31
[44] (Hsu, 1997) p. 165
[45] (Hsu, 1997) p. 211
[46] (Hsu, 1997) p. 83
[47] (Hsu, 1997) p. 98

$$f_{XY}(x,y) = f_X(x)f_Y(y) \qquad \text{2-35}$$

Regression

Regression is a technique used for fitting a set of measured data to a curve. Suppose we want to model the trend of total cost of a program over time. We may measure the cost-to-date at several different times during the program life cycle. Suppose we have N data points and let x_n be the times and y_n be the cost-to-date at time x_n. We may plot these values on a plane, then fit the trend to some predetermined function. Regression analysis is a tool used to find a best fit to the measured data.

One of the most common regression techniques is linear regression. Here, we fit the measured data to a straight line. A general line in the plane is given by

$$y = \alpha x + \beta \qquad \text{2-36}$$

We need to find the best values for α and β. One method for determining α and β would be to minimize the total distance between each data point and the line. This distance is

$$D^2 = \sum_n \frac{(\alpha x_n + \beta - y_n)^2}{1 + \alpha^2} \qquad \text{2-37}$$

and is shown in Figure 2. We would like to find the minimum distance varying α and β. However, this distance leads to complicated expressions and is only viable with numerical analysis.

Instead, we take the approach shown in Figure 3. Here we assume that the independent variable x is an exact measurement and only measure the distance the data points are from the line along the y-axis. In this case the expression for the distance is

$$\chi^2 = \sum_n (\alpha x_n + \beta - y_n)^2. \qquad \text{2-38}$$

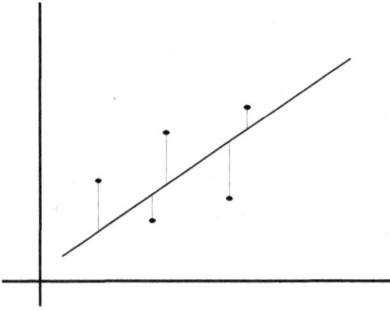

Figure 2: Least-Squares from vertical distance.   Figure 3: Least-Squares from minimum distance.

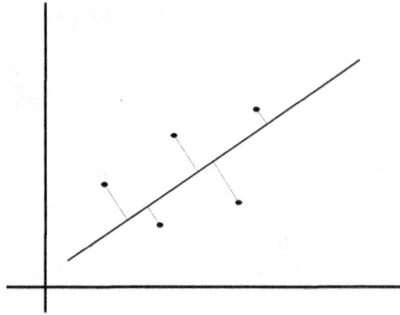

We proceed to optimize this expression with respect to α and β. First, it is useful to define a summation symbol

$$[f_n] = \Sigma_n f_2.$$

2-39

This will make our expressions smaller and easier to manipulate. We begin by optimizing the derivative of χ^2 with respect to α: We set $\frac{\partial \chi^2}{\partial \alpha} = 0$:

$$\frac{\partial \chi^2}{\partial \alpha} = \frac{\partial}{\partial \alpha}[(\alpha x_n + \beta - y_n)^2]$$

2-40

$$= \left[\frac{\partial}{\partial \alpha}(\alpha x_n + \beta - y_n)^2\right]$$

2-41

$$= [2x_n(\alpha x_n + \beta - y_n)]$$

2-42

$$= 2\alpha[x_n{}^2] + 2\beta[x_n] - 2[x_n y_n].$$

2-43

From this, our first equation for optimization is

$$\alpha[x_n{}^2] + \beta[x_n] - [x_n y_n] = 0$$

2-44

We proceed similarly for β setting $\frac{\partial \chi^2}{\partial \beta} = 0$

$$\frac{\partial \chi^2}{\partial \beta} = \frac{\partial}{\partial \beta}[(\alpha x_n + \beta - y_n)^2]$$

2-45

$$= \left[\frac{\partial}{\partial \beta}(\alpha x_n + \beta - y_n)^2\right]$$

2-46

$$= [2(\alpha x_n + \beta - y_n)]$$

2-47

$$= 2\alpha[x_n] + 2\beta[1] - 2[y_n]$$

2-48

$$= 2\alpha[x_n] + 2\beta N - 2[y_n]$$

2-49

or,

$$\alpha[x_n] + \beta N - [y_n] = 0. \tag{2-50}$$

We can simultaneously solve equations 2-44 and 2-50 for α and β,

$$\alpha = \frac{N[x_n y_n] - [x_n][y_n]}{N[x_n{}^2] - [x_n]^2} \tag{2-51}$$

$$\beta = \frac{[y_n][x_n{}^2] - [x_n][x_n y_n]}{N[x_n{}^2] - [x_n]^2} \tag{2-52}$$

These expressions are written in the traditional summation notation as

$$\alpha = \frac{N \sum_n x_n y_n - (\sum_n x_n)(\sum_n y_n)}{N(\sum_n x_n{}^2) - (\sum_n x_n)^2} \tag{2-53}$$

$$\beta = \frac{N(\sum_n y_n)(\sum_n x_n{}^2) - (\sum_n x_n)(\sum_n x_n y_n)}{N(\sum_n x_n{}^2) - (\sum_n x_n)^2} \tag{2-54}$$

This may be written in terms of the variance and covariance,

$$\alpha = \frac{\sigma_{xy}{}^2}{\sigma_x{}^2} \tag{2-55}$$

$$\beta = \bar{y} - \alpha \bar{x} \tag{2-56}$$

A similar process may be carried out to identify best-fits to higher-order polynomials. In general, the regression technique starts with a set of measured data and a model. We then proceed through the following steps:

1. Create an expression for the distance between the measured data points and the model. We do not need to choose distance specifically, but this is a common practice.
2. Take the partial derivative of the distance expression with respect to each model parameter and set this to zero. These result in a set of simultaneous equations we need to satisfy, and there will be one equation for each model parameter.
3. Solve the simultaneous system for the model parameters. Simple models may be solved generally in closed form, as in expressions 2-51 and 2-52. Complicated, non-linear models may require numerical analysis to compute the best-fit model parameters.

It should be noted that the overall model is chosen by the analyst. Regression does not determine the model; rather, it finds the best-fit between the model and the measured data. If we choose a linear model against quadratic measured data, regression will find a fit, but the fit may be very poor.

This technique may be applied to the distance measure in Equation 2-37. This yields the expressions,

$$
(N[x_n y_n] - [x_n][y_n])\alpha^2 \\
+ (N[x_n{}^2] - [x_n]^2 - N[y_n{}^2] + [y_n]^2)\alpha \\
+ [x_n][y_n] - N[x_n y_n] = 0
$$

2-57

$$
\beta = \frac{[y_n] - \alpha[x_n]}{N}
$$

2-58

We can write these in terms of the covariance and variance,

$$
\sigma_{xy}{}^2 \alpha^2 + \left(\sigma_x{}^2 - \sigma_y{}^2\right)\alpha - \sigma_{xy}{}^2 = 0
$$

2-59

$$
\beta = \bar{y} - \alpha\bar{x}
$$

2-60

There are two solutions for α from these equations. One solution is the best-fit where the distance is a minimum. The other is a worst-fit where the distance is a maximum. Once the two values of α are identified, we need to substitute the values for α and β back into Equation 2-37 to determine which is the true best-fit solution.

Application of Tools

As an example of some of these tools in use, we examine the prioritization problem. If the assets only have a single value quantifying them, we can prioritize simply by ranking them against this single value. However, in many non-financial portfolios, the assets will have multiple values.

In this case we cannot simply rank order the assets by value because some assets will be better against one value while worse against another. In addition, the Rationalization Manager often has additional information specifying that certain investments should have similar priorities. This information may come from experience, or may come from the opinions of Executives reviewing the rationalization process.

We need a technique that is capable of combining the multi-valued asset information together to make a prioritized list, while at the same time, accounting for subjective information. Figure 4 shows an example asset data point. Each axis represents some quantifiable information of the asset (cost, number of users, etc.).

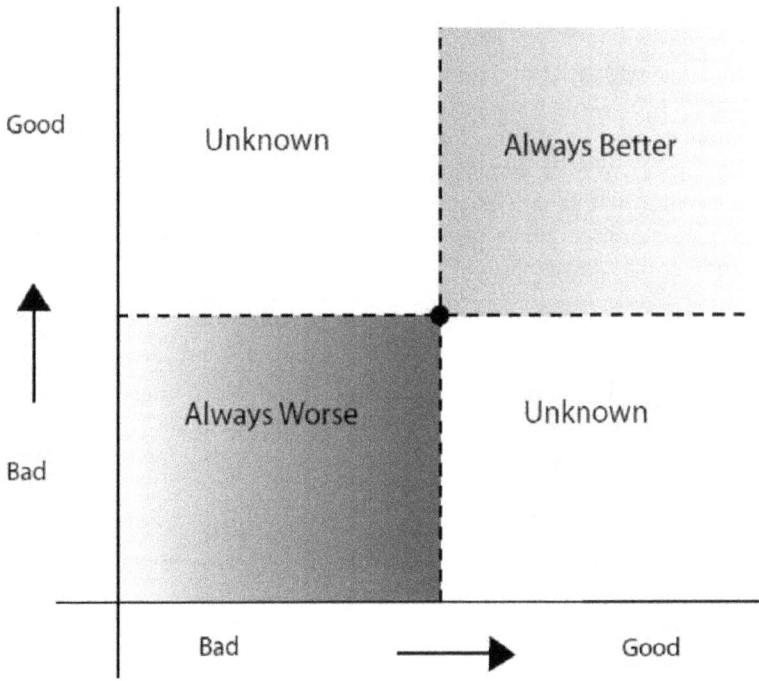

Figure 4: The black dot represents a particular asset data point. Points in the lower-left region are always worse, while points in the upper-right region are always better. Points in the other quadrants do not have a predetermined relation.

It is important to orient all axes the same direction. In the figure, the axes are oriented from bad to good. For example, when quantifying risk, we often have higher values of risk meaning higher risk. Since higher risk is typically bad, we would reverse the axis when plotting against risk in order to have the values run from bad to good.

Assets falling in the upper-right region of Figure 4 are always better than the indicated point. All points in the upper-right region are higher in both axes, so we can safely say that these points must be better. Alternatively, assets falling in the lower-left region are always worse. Here, the values on both axes are always less.

However, the other two regions do not have a definitive comparison. Assets falling into these regions are better with respect to one axis, but worse with respect to the other. We cannot immediately determine how these points relate to the target point. Some will be better, some worse, and others will have the same prioritization value.

We want to use the subjective information at hand to determine how the asset data points relate to each other. We would like to create contours of constant prioritization value that we can plot with the points to determine the relative prioritization of the assets.

We begin with a set of data points in d-dimensions. Let $\vec{P}_n$ be a set of N d-vectors representing the data points. We desire to fit the data points to a parametric family of curves. For example, we could fit a set of 2-vectors to the family $\alpha y + \beta x = \eta$, where α and β are fit parameters, and η is a parameter that generates the family of curves. Generally, an entire family of parametric curves is space filling so there is always some particular member that passes through every data point.

In order to constrain the problem, we assume there are some relations specifying that particular points must lie on the same curve. Let $F(\vec{P}; \vec{\rho}) = \eta$ be the family of curves where $\vec{P}$ is the point in space (the x and y values), while $\vec{\rho}$ is the set of fit parameters (α and β). The set of constraints is represented by

$$F_k(\vec{P}_{1k}; \vec{\rho}) = F_k(\vec{P}_{2k}; \vec{\rho}),$$

2-61

where there are K total constraint relations. In order to find a solution, we must have $K \geq \dim \vec{\rho}$.

Assume that F takes the form

$$F(\vec{P}; \vec{\rho}) = \sum_i \rho_i \sigma^i(\vec{P})$$

2-62

where $\sigma^i(\vec{P})$ is a function of only the spatial coordinates. Let $\sigma^i(\vec{P}_l) \equiv \sigma_l^i$, and use the Einstein summation convention (repeated indices indicate a sum) to rewrite F as

$$F(\vec{P}; \vec{\rho}) = \rho_i \sigma^i$$

2-63

or,

$$F_k(\vec{P}_{1k}; \vec{\rho}) = \rho_i \sigma_{1k}^i.$$

2-64

With this, we can define an optimization function as

$$\chi^2 = \Sigma_k \left(F_k(\vec{P}_{1k}; \vec{\rho}) - F_k(\vec{P}_{2k}; \vec{\rho}) \right)^2.$$

2-65

However, this optimization function is trivially satisfied by $\vec{\rho} = 0$. We can remedy this by fixing any one of the family members to be non-trivial. For instance, if we set $F_1(\vec{P}_{11}; \vec{\rho}) = 1$, this additional constraint is not satisfied by the trivial solution $\vec{\rho} = 0$.

The additional constraint may be added to χ^2 by the method of Lagrange multipliers. The modified χ^2 is

$$\chi^2 = \sum_k \left(F_k(\vec{P}_{1k};\vec{\rho}) - F_k(\vec{P}_{2k};\vec{\rho}) \right)^2$$

2-66

$$+ 2\lambda\left(F_1(\vec{P}_{11};\vec{\rho}) - 1 \right)$$

$$= \sum_k \left(\rho_i \sigma_{1k}^i - \rho_i \sigma_{2k}^i \right)^2 + 2\lambda\left(\rho_i \sigma_{11}^i - 1 \right)$$

2-67

We optimize χ^2 by taking the partial derivative with respect to each of the parameters and setting the result to zero:

$$\frac{\partial \chi^2}{\partial \rho_j} = 2 \sum_k \left(\rho_i \sigma_{1k}^i - \rho_i \sigma_{2k}^i \right)\left(\sigma_{1k}^j - \sigma_{2k}^j \right) + 2\lambda\sigma_{11}^j = 0$$

2-68

$$\frac{\partial \chi^2}{\partial \lambda} = 2\left(\rho_i \sigma_{11}^i - 1 \right) = 0$$

2-69

These equations can be simplified to,

$$\rho_i \left(\sigma_{1k}^i - \sigma_{2k}^i \right)\left(\sigma_{1k}^j - \sigma_{2k}^j \right) + \lambda\sigma_{11}^j = 0$$

2-70

$$\rho_i \sigma_{11}^i = 1$$

2-71

where we have used the summation convention for the sum over k.

These equations are a system of linear equations in terms of the fit parameters and λ. In matrix form,

$$\begin{pmatrix} \left(\sigma_{1k}^i - \sigma_{2k}^i \right)\left(\sigma_{1k}^j - \sigma_{2k}^j \right) & \cdots & \sigma_{11}^j \\ \vdots & \ddots & \vdots \\ \sigma_{11}^i & \cdots & 0 \end{pmatrix} \begin{pmatrix} \vec{\rho} \\ \lambda \end{pmatrix} = \begin{pmatrix} 0 \\ \vdots \\ 1 \end{pmatrix}$$

2-72

or,

$$\mathcal{M}\vec{\psi} = \vec{\omega}$$

2-73

where

$$\mathcal{M} = \begin{pmatrix} \left(\sigma_{1k}^i - \sigma_{2k}^i \right)\left(\sigma_{1k}^j - \sigma_{2k}^j \right) & \cdots & \sigma_{11}^j \\ \vdots & \ddots & \vdots \\ \sigma_{11}^i & \cdots & 0 \end{pmatrix}$$

2-74

and $\vec{\psi} = \begin{pmatrix} \vec{\rho} \\ \lambda \end{pmatrix}$, $\vec{\omega} = \begin{pmatrix} 0 \\ \vdots \\ 1 \end{pmatrix}$.

This system is formally solved by multiplying by $\mathcal{M}^{-1}$,

$$\vec{\psi} = \mathcal{M}^{-1}\vec{\omega}.$$

2-75

Figure 5 provides an example of asset data plotted in two dimensions.

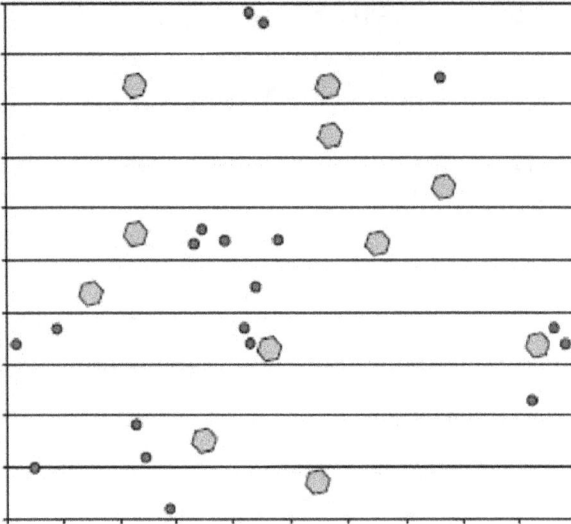

Figure 5: Initial example data for prioritization. Diamonds and triangles represent asset data points. Triangles are data points that are matched by subjective rules.

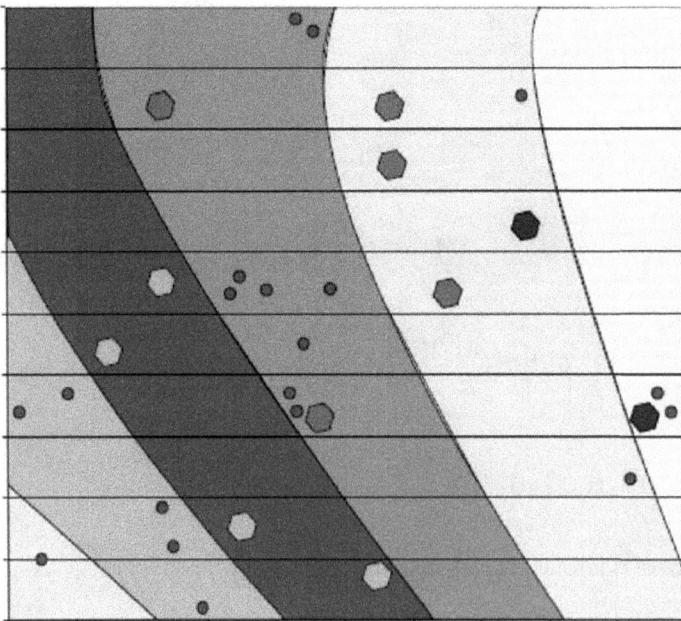

Figure 6: Contour from fitting the data using the subjective analysis. Colored regions are areas with similar prioritization values.

Subjective prioritizations are presented as triangular data points. Triangles with matching colors are subjectively considered to have the same prioritization.

We apply Equation 2-74 to the data from Figure 5 to get a contour fit. The fit is shown in Figure 6. Each colored region indicates assets with similar priority values.

Note the right pair of assets in Figure 6. These assets are subjectively considered the same; however, they appear in different bands. This is the nature of curve fitting routines. There is no guarantee that a pair of constrained points will in fact be equal in the fit. The fit is combining the subjective specifications of the relative fits with an objective numerical method.

This approach has the drawback that the contours obtained from the optimization procedure may connect points that are ordered by the coordinate system. For example, a contour passing through the lower-left and upper-right regions of Figure 4 would imply that some points from the lower-left region have the same value as points from the upper-right region. But from the coordinate system, we know that all points in the upper-right region are higher value than all points of the lower-left region.

We can constrain the contours from the optimization by requiring that the contours do not connect points from the lower-left and upper-right regions. This leads to an additional constraint of the form

$$\sum_{i \neq j} \frac{\partial F\left(\vec{P}; \vec{\rho}\right)}{\partial x_i} \frac{\partial F\left(\vec{P}; \vec{\rho}\right)}{\partial x_j} \geq 0 \qquad \text{2-76}$$

Constraints such as this may be handled by nonlinear programming methods and the Karush-Kuhn-Tucker conditions.

3 Portfolio Rationalization Process

Portfolio rationalization is carried out in a series of steps starting with a snapshot of the investments and culminating with recommendations for rationalization.

Figure 7 shows the series of high-level phases in the process of portfolio rationalization. However, it should be understood that these phases do not need to be strictly sequential. Rather, they may be performed in parallel and potentially in different orders. We will address this further when we discuss the portfolio rationalization life cycle.

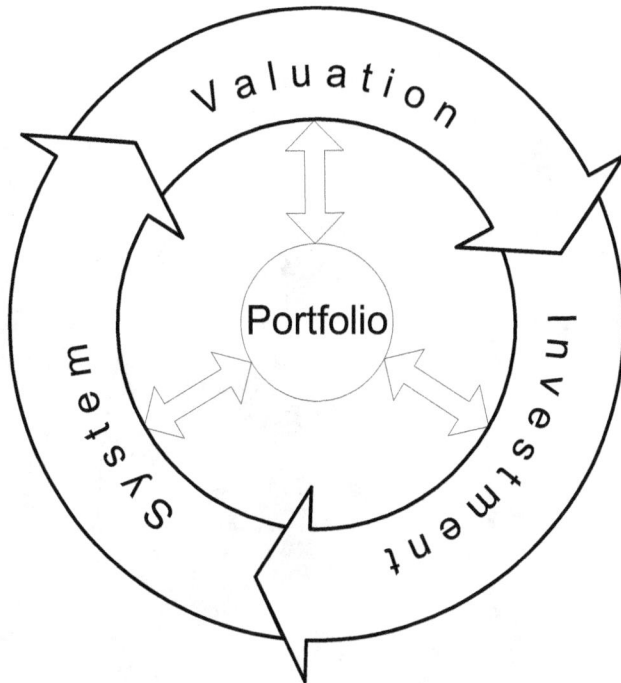

Figure 7: Portfolio rationalization as a series of phases. Valuation, Investment, and System Analysis are steps in a cycle of analysis that support the Portfolio Analysis process.

Portfolio rationalization is divided into four main phases. Each of these high-level phases is broken down to more detailed processes. Figure 9 shows a diagram indicating some more detailed processes in the Portfolio Rationalization Process. The high-level phases and their processes are explained below.

Each of the four main phases culminates in a mathematical model used to quantify the business value for the phase. The Valuation phase yields the Valuation Model, the Investment phase provides the Investment Model, the System Phase gives the System Model, and the Portfolio phase has the Portfolio Model. Each of these models examines a separate aspect of the valuation of the portfolio. In addition, the Rationalization Model examines the portfolio of investments to identify rationalization targets and organizational best practices.

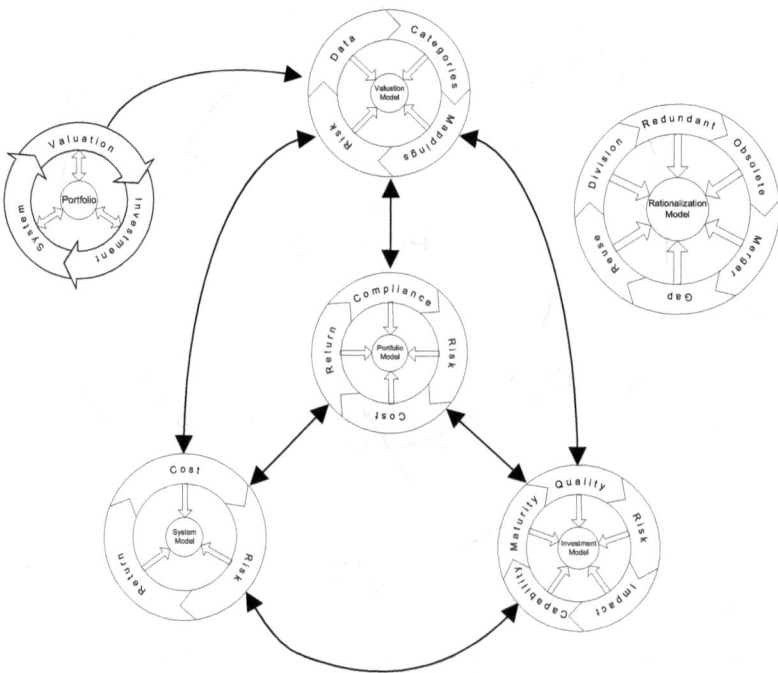

Figure 8: Portfolio rationalization phases along with the Valuation Mode, Investment Model, System model, Portfolio Model. and Rationalization Model.

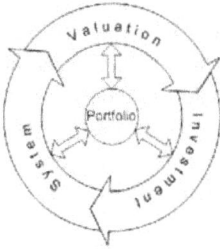

The Portfolio Rationalization lifecycle is a continuous, ongoing operation, not a linear procedure. Information enters the lifecycle as raw data in the Valuation phase, then proceeds to the Investment phase, then the System phase, and finally the Portfolio phase. The culmination of the lifecycle is the identification of Best Practices and Rationalization Targets.

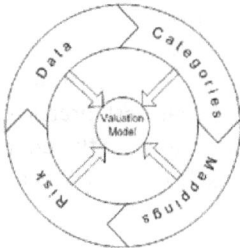

The Valuation Model analyzes the available raw investment information to produce a set of mathematical models that may be used to compute the business value of the investments. The Valuation Model does not compute the actual business values. Instead, this model provides the fundamental mathematical relations that may be used to compute business value.

The Investment Model uses the results from the Valuation Model to compute the business value for each of the investments. The Investment Model provides a mathematical relationship to compute every identified business value for each of the investments. This model is fundamental to the portfolio rationalization process.

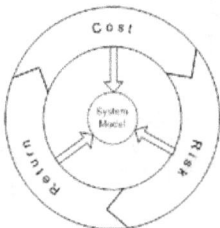

The System Model examines the investments at a system level. Investments may be grouped together for a coherent purpose similar to how a set of projects may form a program. When a group of investments is choreographed to together as a whole, the overall value of the system may be greater than the sum of its parts. The System Model examines this and provides mathematical models to identify the additional benefits the system of investment obtains in excess of the sum of the constituent investments.

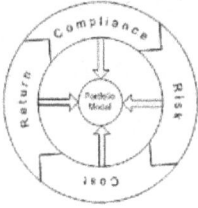

The Portfolio Model reviews the portfolio as a whole and identifies additional value from the alignment of the individual investments and systems with the strategic direction of the portfolio. The alignment of the investments with the strategic direction can produce additional value for the portfolio.

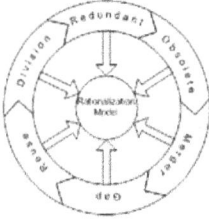

The Rationalization Model uses the results of the previous models to create a system of rules used to determine which investments require rationalization. In addition to these rationalization targets, the Rationalization Model identifies organizational best practices. This information may be used to drive the entire portfolio toward increasing levels of efficiency and value.

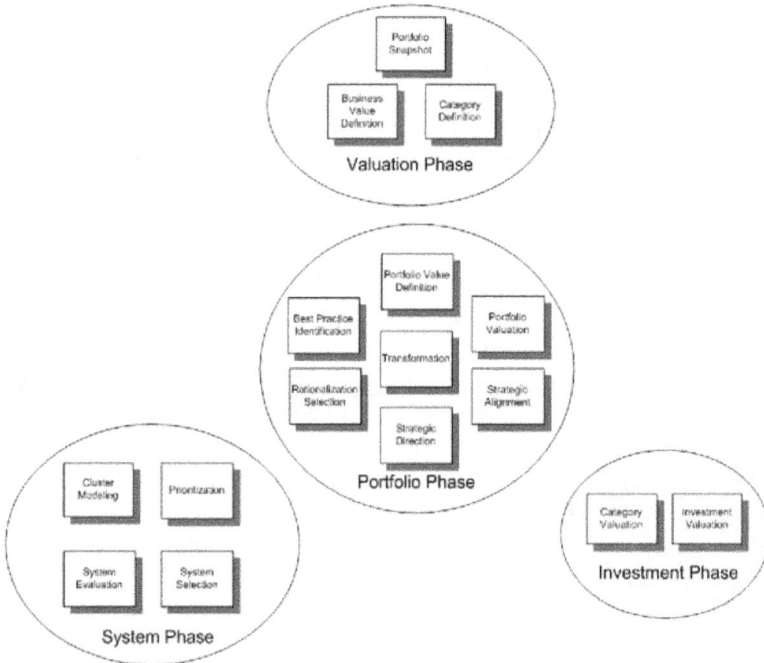

Figure 9: The portfolio rationalization process.

Tailoring the Process

It is important to note that the process and flows detailed here are not intended to be used for every rationalization effort. We present common processes that may be incorporated into an overall rationalization process. Each rationalization effort should review these processes and identify the specific processes and practices that are most appropriate to that effort.

Tailoring the rationalization process means choosing a particular set of processes for use in a given rationalization effort. The Rationalization Manager should use their judgment to determine which of these processes are appropriate and add the most value.

Initially, a simplified process may be put in place. The Rationalization Manager may begin with a simple process, and then add processes as the organization becomes more acquainted with portfolio rationalization. This approach allows the organization to reap some benefits of portfolio rationalization without the cost of setting up a lengthy structure. In addition, this approach allows the Rationalization Manager to identify and add processes that have the greatest impact on the performance of the portfolio.

Over time, additional processes or additional detail may be added to existing processes. As an organization sees the value of the Portfolio Rationalization Process, adding more detail may be beneficial. This is especially true as the portfolio becomes better aligned with the organizational strategy and begins to create increasing benefits with decreasing costs.

Some parts of the process are routine and may be automated. Organizations may gain value by implementing automated portfolio management practices. One of the goals of the process described here is to migrate toward a fully automated and integrated procedure. At this point, the process may run using only some overall monitor and control, with Executives and Portfolio Managers automatically receiving reports and notifications as the portfolio evolves.

Valuation

The Valuation phase is the beginning of the Portfolio Rationalization Lifecycle. This phase identifies the methodologies used to value the portfolio investments. The culmination of this phase is the Valuation Model, which is used for the valuation of the portfolio investments. The Investment Model is comprised of a set of technical guidelines and data that provide a means to relatively value each asset. The methodology enables each asset to be ranked with respect to the other assets. This partially ordered ranking structure will continue throughout the rationalization lifecycle.

Portfolio Snapshot
1. Asset Information
1. Portfolio Snapshot
1. Data Repositories 2. Status Reports 3. Field Investigations 4. Interviews 5. Questionnaires

Category Definition
1. Portfolio Snapshot
1. Investment Categories
1. Data Analysis

Business Value Definition
1. Portfolio Snapshot
2. Investment Categories
1. Valuation Model
2. Relational Categories
3. IR Category Maps
1. Risk Analysis
2. Mathematical Models
3. Numerical Methods
4. Statistical Techniques
5. Requirements Analysis

Figure 10: Portfolio Snapshot process Inputs, Outputs, and Tools & Techniques.

Figure 11: Category Definition process Inputs, Outputs, and Tools & Techniques.

Figure 12: Business Value Definition process Inputs, Outputs, and Tools & Techniques.

Figure 10-Figure 12 detail the processes of the Valuation phase. In each figure we have a diagram showing the process name, inputs, outputs, and tools and techniques. Each of the Portfolio Rationalization Processes is diagrammed similarly in the figures in the following sections.

Portfolio Snapshot

The Portfolio Snapshot is a collection of investment data taken at a particular instant. This data provides a basis for understanding what information is available for the asset and the quality of the data. The quality of the data is important to the valuation of the investment because data quality helps measure the uncertainty in the business valuation. For example, if we realize that the data supporting a particular investment is changing rapidly, there is a high uncertainty in the measurement of the business value. This uncertainty must be incorporated into our analysis in order to produce reliable results.

The Portfolio Snapshot is a compilation of Asset Information. The data may come from a data repository, status reports, field investigations, management interviews, questionnaires, etc. Regardless of the data source, the Portfolio Snapshot compiles all of this information together at a single location. This data repository will be used by other processes in portfolio rationalization.

The main output of the Portfolio Snapshot process is the Portfolio Snapshot. This data set is used throughout portfolio rationalization and plays a key role in all of the other processes and phases. Typically, the Portfolio Snapshot process is regularly repeated in order to keep the data up-to-date during the life cycle of portfolio rationalization.

Category Definition

Category definition is another process executed for Valuation Analysis. Here, a set of categories that cover all investments is defined. For example, we may choose 'Program Budget' as a particular category. As such, we may bin the 'Program Budget' into one of four bins: below $1M, between $1M and $10M, between $10M and $100M, and over $100M. Under this paradigm, the 'Program Budget' category takes on one of four values. Every investment may be given a specific value for this category.

It is usually preferable to have categories with a discrete set of values as opposed to a continuous value. In the example above, we took a continuous variable, the 'Program Budget', and made it into a discrete variable, the category value, by setting a series of thresholds. This is useful because the category values for each investment will later be used to perform cluster modeling on the investments. The cluster modeling process does work with continuous variables; however, it is often easier to work with discrete variables.

Category Definition depends on the Portfolio Snapshot process. A list of potential data fields is created when making the Portfolio Snapshot. Moreover, the snapshot data will provide insight into which fields are and are not reliably populated. This information can be used during the Category Definition process to evaluate the utility used to create a category from a specific field or combination of fields.

The main output of the Category Definition process is the Investment Categories. The selection of categories is accomplished by analyzing the data found in the Portfolio Snapshot. These categories are a fundamental input to the Valuation Model and are part of the basis of Business Value.

Business Value Definition

This process specifies the Mathematical Models and Numerical Methods that will be used to quantify the business value of an asset and the associated uncertainty (risk). The Business Valuation Definition process is dependent on the output of the Category Definition process. The business value is typically a mathematical function combining some set of categories. As such, this process needs to know what categories are available for use in determining the business value.

A simple approach is to use the category values for the asset and create a weighted sum to obtain the business value:

$$B = \sum_i w_i c_i \qquad \text{3-1}$$

In the above expression, B is the business value, w_i is the weight associated with the ith category, and c_i is the value of the ith category.

The weights w_i may be simply set by hand, or may be computed through a regression analysis on the data. The regression analysis may be performed by creating a partially ordered relative ranking of the investments, then performing a least-squares regression to fit the specified values to a linear model.

In addition to specifying a model for the value of an investment, it is equally important to evaluate the uncertainty in the value. As an example, if an investment has a value of $1M, it is important to know if the measurement is $1M±$0.1M or $1M±$0.0001M. These uncertainties can make a difference in the relative ranking of the investments. We need to be more careful when we have business values with high uncertainties. Otherwise, we may recommend making a change to an investment believing it has a certain value when in fact the investment has a significantly different value. In this case, we may inadvertently make incorrect recommendations for the investment.

The business valuation is perhaps the most complicated and most important process for portfolio rationalization. This particular process specifies the model(s) that will be used to determine business value. These models form the Investment Model. We will discuss the Investment Model in more detail in Section 5.

Investment

The Investment phase examines each asset, determines the asset category values, and computes the business value. This process is essential to portfolio rationalization as this is the process where we arrive at a business value for each asset. Later phases will use the results of the Investment phase to create Investment Clusters and examine the performance of the portfolio as a whole.

The Investment phase has two main processes: Category Valuation and Investment Valuation. Category Valuation specifies the values for the asset categories, while Investment Valuation computes the business value. This phase is dependent on the Valuation Phase, as that phase determines what the categories are, the allowed category values, and how the business value is computed.

Category Valuation

Category Valuation is the process of determining the value of each category for every investment. For example, an investment may be categorized as: 'Program Budget' = $1M-$10M, 'Criticality' = High, 'Number of Users' ≤ 500, etc. This process examines each investment and determines the value for each of the categories.

Category Valuation
1. Portfolio Snapshot
2. Investment Categories
3. Relational Categories
4. IR Category Maps
1. Asset Category Data
1. Data Repositories
2. Status Reports
3. Field Investigations
4. Interviews
5. Questionnaires

Figure 13: Category Valuation process Inputs, Outputs, and Tools & Techniques.

Investment Valuation
1. Relational Categories
2. Valuation Model
3. Asset Category Data
1. Investment Model
2. Investment Valuations
1. Computational Intelligence
2. Numerical Methods
3. Mathematical Models

Figure 14: Investment Valuation process Inputs, Outputs, and Tools & Techniques.

The list of categories and allowed values is determined in the Category Definition process of the Valuation phase. The Category Valuation process is the point where the category values are actually specified for every asset. The actual values for each investment are determined by examining the data in the Portfolio Snapshot. In this respect, the Category Valuation process is dependent on both the Portfolio Snapshot and Category Definition processes.

The Category Valuation process may be completed using a variety of methods. Optimally, the Category Valuation process uses the information from the Portfolio Snapshot to compute the values using a database repository that is reliably kept up-to-date. Alternatively, the Category Valuation process may use status reports, field investigations, interviews, or questionnaires to determine the category value for a specific investment.

The Category Valuation process computes the values for both the Investment Categories as well as the Relational Categories. This combined set of category data makes up the Asset Category Data that is the output of this process.

Investment Valuation

Investment Valuation is the process of computing the business value for every investment. The business value is computed from the Investment Model. The business value of the assets is an essential measurement that is used throughout portfolio rationalization. The business value is computed using the results of the Category Valuation process as well as the Business Valuation Definition. The Category Valuation process provides the raw data required, while the Business Valuation Definition provides the Investment Model which specifies the Numerical Methods and

Mathematical Models used to compute the business value. Because of these relationships, the Investment Valuation process is dependent on the Category Valuation and Business Valuation Definition processes.

It is important to note that the business value has two components: a measurement and an uncertainty. For example, the value $1M±$0.1M has measured value $1M and uncertainty $0.1M. Each of these numbers is meaningless in isolation. Simply stating that a measurement has a value of $1M does not by itself convey any useful information. If the measurement is $1M±$100M, the measurement is all but useless. Similarly, stating that a measurement is made with an uncertainty of ±$5M tells us nothing about the value of the measurement. It is the combination of these that makes a value useful.

Furthermore, there may be more than one business value for each investment. This is useful when assets have different value aspects which are simply not comparable. For example, a portfolio may have the majority of assets with an assigned ROI. However, there may be a few compliance assets that do not have a ROI because these investments are related to mandatory compliance issues.

One approach may be to assign an extremely high business value to the compliance investments in order to guarantee that their value is higher than all other investments. Although this may achieve the desired goal, it may also lead to a skewed analysis of the investments. The fundamental problem here is that the ROI value is simply not comparable to the mandatory compliance value.

A better method may be to have two business values: one related to ROI and another related to mandatory compliance. In this case the ROI assets will have a low or zero value for mandatory compliance, but a measureable ROI. Moreover, the compliance investments will have a low ROI but a high compliance value. In this respect the investments may be analyzed differently but using the same overall methodology.

System

The System phase of portfolio rationalization examines groupings or clusters of investments. This phase identifies groups of assets with similar properties in order to facilitate the rapid identification of high-performing investments as well as problem areas.

In addition, the groups are assigned a business value apart from the cumulative value of the constituent investments. The value of the group may be the same of the sum of the constituent investments, or it may be greater or less.

The System Phase is comprised of four processes: Cluster Modeling, Prioritization, System Selection, and System Evaluation. These processes group similar investments, identify systems of interest, and gather detailed information on the systems of interest.

This phase begins with Cluster Modeling, which is the process of grouping together investments that have similar properties. Then the Prioritization Process is used to rank order the performance of the assets so that problem investments may be addressed in more detail. System Selection is used to choose specific systems for detailed examination. Finally, the System Evaluation process is used to examine the system in detail and obtain specific System Requirements.

Cluster Modeling

The Cluster Modeling process groups investments together using their category values or other characteristics that may be used to identify similar investments. The specific category values for each investment are determined in the Category Valuation process during the Investment phase.

The input to the Cluster Modeling process is the Asset Category Data from the Categorization Process. In most cases, we wish to analyze many categories simultaneously. We can use standard charts to analyze up to three categories at a time: a single category can be plotted on a line, two categories can be graphed in a plane, and three categories may be plotted in space. However, when we have more than three dimensions, there is no efficient method to represent all of the data at the same time.

Thus, cluster modeling problems often become a multi-dimensional Data Analysis problem. These problems are difficult to analyze by hand as there is no simple way to visualize the information. In these cases it is often useful to resort to an automated computer analysis using special software systems designed to analyze multi-dimensional data.

Because of this, cluster modeling is best performed with numerical analysis software and algorithms. Furthermore, computationally intelligent software systems provide an efficient means to determine the Investment Clusters. These software systems are able to analyze this multi-dimensional data quickly and accurately and arrive at clusters that are difficult to determine using a manual process.

The product of the Cluster Modeling process is a grouping of investments into clusters. The clusters represent groups of assets that have similar properties. This grouping is useful because it can quickly identify entire groups of investments that are performing effectively and groups that are problematic.

These problem groups are of particular interest in portfolio rationalization and will be further examined in later processes.

Prioritization

Prioritization is the process of rank ordering the current portfolio assets according to their overall performance, and rank ordering potential new investments. The Prioritization process is dependent on the Cluster Modeling process in order to identify groups of investments that are collectively underperforming. In addition, Prioritization is also dependent on the Valuation process as the investment value may be used to assist in the rank ordering of the investments.

A fitness score is computed for each investment in question. For the current portfolio investments, the fitness score should reflect the overall asset performance based on the business value and risk as determined in the Investment Valuation process. Fitness is also computed for potential new investments. The fitness should reflect both the estimated business value of an investment as well as the associated risk.

Cluster Modeling
1. Asset Category Data 2. Investment Values
1. Investment Clusters
1. Computational Intelligence 2. Numerical Methods 3. Mathematical Models

Figure 15: Cluster Modeling process Inputs, Outputs, and Tools & Techniques.

Prioritization
1. Investment Values 2. Investment Clusters
1. Prioritized Investments
1. Fitness Models 2. Risk Analysis 3. Computational Intelligence 4. Numerical Methods 5. Mathematical Models

Figure 16: Prioritization process Inputs, Outputs, and Tools & Techniques.

System Selection
1. Investment Values 2. Investment Clusters 3. Prioritized Investments
1. System Selection Criteria 2. Selected Systems
1. Fitness Models 2. Risk Analysis 3. Computational Intelligence 4. Numerical Methods 5. Mathematical Models 6. Quad Charts

Figure 17: System Selection process Inputs, Outputs, and Tools & Techniques.

System Evaluation
1. Selected Systems 2. System Requirements
1. System Evaluations 2. System Model 3. System Business Values
1. Requirements Gathering 2. Use Case Models 3. Interviews 4. Questionnaires 5. Field Investigations

Figure 18: System Evaluation process Inputs, Outputs, and Tools & Techniques.

The output of the Prioritization process is a rank ordering of the current assets according to their overall performance, and a rank ordering of potential portfolio additions according to their fitness. In each case, fitness is determined by a combination of the business value, the identification of the asset into a particular cluster, and the associated investment risk.

System Selection

The System Selection process determines a list of investments for deeper investigation based on the rankings from Prioritization. This process examines the Investment Values and Investment Clusters, along with the lists of prioritized assets, to identify potential selection criteria for rationalization. The selection of investments as candidates for rationalization narrows the focus from the entire portfolio of investments to a selected set of investments. These selected investments are investigated further in the Portfolio phase.

The System Selection process does not produce a list of investments that *should* be rationalized. Rather, this process identifies the investments, when analyzed individually or according to their clusters, that appear to be potential Rationalization Targets. However, the Portfolio phase will make a final determination of investments for rationalization.

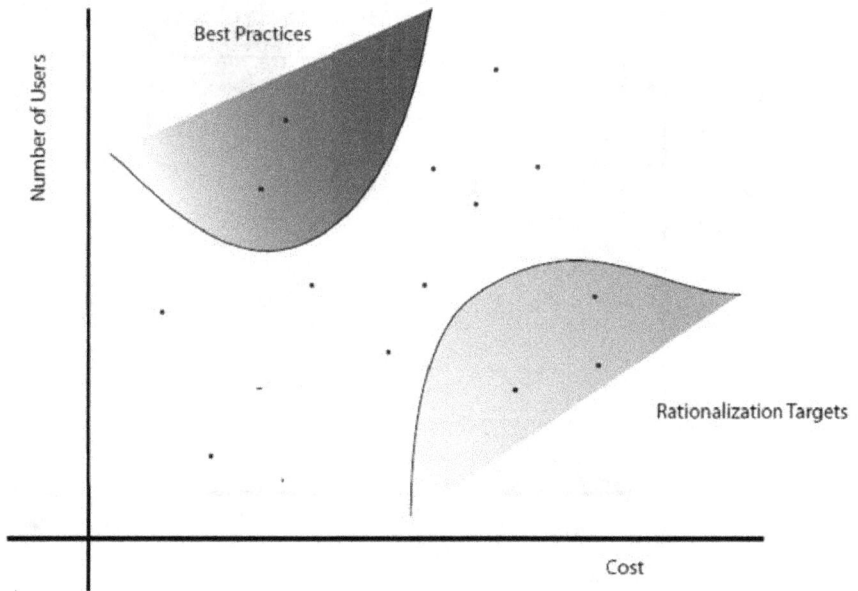

Figure 19: Rationalization Targets and Best Practices

The output of the System Selection process is a set of System Selection Criteria and Selected Systems. The System Selection Criteria is determined by reviewing the Investment Values and Clusters with the Prioritized Assets. Each Investment Cluster is examined and ranked by the Investment Value. Typically, a cutoff value is determined by weighing the grouping of the Investment Values, the number of investments above/below the cutoff, and the amount of time required to analyze the selected investments. The investments on one side of the cutoff (above/below) make up the Selected Systems, while the remaining investments are considered weak rationalization targets.

A given investment may be in more than one Cluster. It may be the case that a specific investment is a weak rationalization target in one Cluster but a strong rationalization target in another Cluster. This demonstrates the multi-dimensional nature of non-financial investments and the utility of multiple Business Values. Assets demonstrating these characteristics should be carefully examined to assure that a rationalization of the investment does not do more harm where the portfolio is strong than good from rationalization where the portfolio is weak.

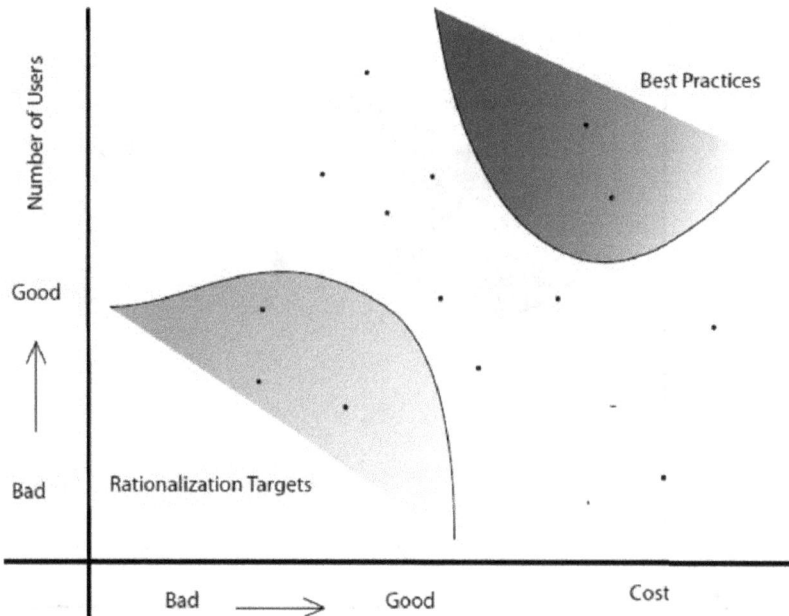

Figure 20: Rationalization Targets and Best Practices in quad chart standard form.

System Evaluation

The System Evaluation process examines the selected investments from the System Selection process. System Requirements, purpose, and functionality are detailed and documented. Requirements documentation may be completed by utilizing use cases to specify the various requirements. The use cases may then be diagrammed in a use case model.

The first output of the System Evaluation process is the System Model. This model analyzes groups of related assets and identifies the value of the system as a whole. The composite value may be different that the sum of the values of the individual investments. This value may be greater than the sum of the individuals, indicating that the investments work coherently together as a group to produce a greater value. Alternatively, the value may be less than the sum of the constituents, indicating that the system has redundant or overlapping components.

The second output of this process is the detailed System Evaluations. These requirements are examined during the Portfolio phase to identify redundancy, obsolescence, investment merger and division opportunities, opportunities for reuse, and requirements gaps. Detailed analysis of these requirements provides the means for identifying assets that are good candidates for rationalization.

The final output is the System Business Values. Here, a Business Value is assigned to every system of investments. The Business Value need not be simply the sum of the Business Values of the constituent investments. In fact, the System Business Value may have Business Values for categories that are not even present in any of the investments comprising the system.

When the System Business Value is greater than the sum of the constituent investments, the system is seen as operating with increased utility due to the interaction of the system investments. This is reflected in the concept that 'the whole is greater than the sum of its parts.' These systems are enhanced through the efficient interaction of the individual investments working together to provide value above and beyond the simple sum of the individual investment values.

Alternatively, the System Business Value may be less than the sum of the constituent investments. In this case, the investments may create friction with each other. For example, a system of investments that feed information from one investment to another in an accounting process may require substantial manual intervention in order to function properly. This intervention may be viewed as a reduction in value to the system.

System selection often uses quad charts to graphically present assets according to a two-variable valuation. Two asset valuation values are chosen and a group of investments are plotted accordingly.

For example, we may choose 'cost' and 'number of users'. Plotting 'cost' on the x-axis and 'number of users' on the y-axis, we may arrive at a graph similar to Figure 19. Here, assets in the upper left region are high 'cost' and low 'number of users'. This region would be of interest to examine as these assets appear to provide little bang-for-the-buck.

However, the assets in the lower right region are of interest as well. These assets are low 'cost' and high 'number of users'. These assets should be examined as they appear to provide high impact with little cost. Investments in this region should be examined to identify organizational Best Practices.

Figure 19 also demonstrates a typical problem with quad charts. The y-axis, 'number of users', increases from bottom to top. Increasing 'number of users' is typically desirable as the more users there are to a system, the more valuable the system becomes. Alternatively, the x-axis, 'cost', increases as well, but increasing cost is not typically more desirable.

Hence, the y-axis appears to run from bad to good while the x-axis runs from good to bad. When creating quad charts, it is advisable to identify a 'desired state' and order the axes so that the desired state is at the upper right while the least desired state is at the lower left. Consistently putting quad charts in this standard form helps the audience to quickly understand the information in the quad chart. Figure 20 shows the chart from Figure 19 in standard form.

Portfolio

The Portfolio phase focuses on analyzing the portfolio as a whole and makes recommendations for investment rationalization. This is distinct from the System phase because although the System phase examines groups of investments, it does not analyze the portfolio as a whole. The Portfolio phase represents the culmination of portfolio rationalization and results in specific recommendations for investment action.

This phase is divided into seven processes: Portfolio Value Definition, Portfolio Valuation, Strategic Alignment, Strategic Direction, Rationalization Selection, Best Practice Identification, and Transformation. Essentially, these processes assess where the portfolio currently stands, where we want it to be, and how we are going to get there.

The Portfolio Value Definition process is similar to the Business Valuation Definition process but applies to the portfolio as a whole rather than the individual investments. The Portfolio Value Definition process creates a Portfolio Model similar to the Investment Model from the Business Valuation Definition process.

Portfolio Valuation is similar to Investment Valuation. In this process, the portfolio is assigned one or more values which are used to measure the overall performance of the portfolio. This process may implement Computational Intelligence, Numerical Methods, or Mathematical Models to value and measure the portfolio.

The Strategic Alignment process analyzes the portfolio investments and clusters to determine how well each is aligned to the Business Strategy and Business Vision. The Strategic Alignment process determines the current state of the portfolio and how well the overall portfolio is aligned with the business goals, which areas are well aligned, and which areas are misaligned. This process represents the concept 'Here is where we are.'

The Strategic Direction process examines the portfolio investments and identifies specific target goals and future directions for the portfolio. Specifically, the Strategic Direction specifies the desired future state for the portfolio. This process represents the concept 'This is where we want to be.'

The Rationalization Selection process identifies specific investments as rationalization targets. Rationalization Selection examines the Business Strategy and Vision, the Portfolio Valuation and Performance, System Evaluations, and Strategic Alignments and Recommendations to determine the appropriate investments for rationalization.

Best Practice Identification discovers the investments that are performing well and determines the fundamental reasons for their performance. This leads to the identification of organizational Best Practices. These Best Practices may be applied to other investments to improve the overall performance of the portfolio.

The Transformation process develops a detailed plan for how the portfolio will reach the desired future state. This is an action plan providing specific recommendations for changes to particular investments. Moreover, this plan demonstrates how these recommendations will help to achieve the desired future portfolio state. This process represents the concept 'How we are going to get there.'

Portfolio Value Definition

The Portfolio Value Definition process specifies the Mathematical Models, Numerical Methods, and/or Computational Intelligence techniques used to measure the performance and uncertainty of the portfolio. The portfolio value(s) are specified as one or more numbers with their associated uncertainties.

The Portfolio Value Definition uses the Business Strategy and Vision along with the Investment Model and System Evaluations to determine the Portfolio Model. The Business Strategy and Vision are used as a guide to identify which aspects of the portfolio are most important to quantify. As the portfolio value is based on the business values of the investments in the portfolio, the portfolio value requires an understanding of the Investment Model. Finally, the System Evaluations are used to determine the potential areas of interest for quantifying the values with respect to the requirements.

Based on these inputs, the Portfolio Value Definition process specifies the Portfolio Model. The Portfolio Model is chosen to reflect the various measures that may be used to compute the performance of the portfolio as a whole based on the individual Investment Values. The Portfolio Model is discussed in further detail in Section 7.

Portfolio Valuation

Portfolio Valuation is the process of quantifying the value of the portfolio and determining the Portfolio Performance. This process computes the portfolio value(s) by applying the Portfolio Model to the Investment Values, taking into account the Business Strategy, Business Vision, and Investment Values.

Portfolio Valuation may use analysis techniques such as Computational Intelligence, Numerical Methods, and Mathematical Models. These are valuable techniques for understanding the complex interactions between the investments that comprise the portfolio.

Portfolio Value Definition
1. Business Strategy
2. Business Vision
3. Investment Model
4. System Evaluations
5. System Model
6. System Business Values
7. Performance Expectations
8. Statutes & Regulations
1. Portfolio Model
1. Alignment Models
2. Performance Models
3. Risk Models
4. Taxation Issues
5. Requirements Analysis

Portfolio Valuation
1. Portfolio Model
2. Business Strategy
3. Business Vision
4. System Evaluations
5. System Business Values
6. Investment Values
1. Portfolio Valuation
2. Portfolio Performance
1. Computational Intelligence
2. Numerical Methods
3. Mathematical Models
4. System Diagrams

Strategic Alignment
1. Business Strategy
2. Business Vision
3. System Evaluations
4. System Business Values
1. Strategic Alignments
1. Alignment Models
2. Performance Models
3. Risk Analysis

Figure 21: Portfolio Value Definition process Inputs, Outputs, and Tools & Techniques.

Figure 22: Portfolio Valuation process Inputs, Outputs, and Tools & Techniques.

Figure 23: Strategic Alignment process Inputs, Outputs, and Tools & Techniques.

The outputs of the Portfolio Valuation process are the actual Portfolio Valuation and the Portfolio Performance. There are a wide variety of techniques that may be used to compute the values, uncertainties, and performance of the investment portfolio. The Portfolio Model specifies the particular set of valuation techniques to compute.

Strategic Alignment

The Strategic Alignment process analyzes the portfolio investments to identify areas that are aligned with the Business Vision and areas that are not. The Business Strategy is a statement of the business mission, vision, and objectives. The Business Vision is a particular portion of the Business Strategy specifically targeted toward the desired future state of the business. The Strategic Alignment process evaluates the current and potential new investments to determine how well these investments are aligned with the Business Strategy and Vision.

The Strategic Alignment process depends on the Cluster Modeling process of the System Analysis phase. The investment groupings identified by the Cluster Modeling process are used to evaluate how well groups of investments are aligned with the overall Business Strategy. Moreover, these groupings can be used to determine how well asset groups are aligned with the Business Vision.

This process also determines the overall performance of the portfolio as a whole. The performance measure may be as simple as profit or ROI, or it may be a more complicated model accounting for the strategic value of individual assets. In any case, one main output of the Strategic Alignment process is an evaluation of the overall Portfolio Performance, the performance of asset clusters, and the performance of individual investments.

In this manner, the Strategic Alignment process is able to assess how well the portfolio is currently performing. The performance may be measured simply on the basis of overall ROI, or the performance may be evaluated in more complicated terms, weighing the Strategic Alignment of the investments.

Strategic Direction

The Strategic Direction process reviews the cluster model, investment prioritization, and investments selected for rationalization to evaluate which investments are performing well and identify problem assets. In addition, the Strategic Direction process also incorporates the Business Strategy and Vision into its analysis to determine what changes should be made to the portfolio in order to achieve the vision.

The Strategic Direction process depends on the Cluster Modeling process and the Prioritization process. The Cluster Modeling process is important because the cluster model identifies groups of investments with similar properties. This grouping is useful to quickly identify problem areas within the portfolio. Prioritization is important because the prioritized lists of current and potential assets may be used to measure how well these assets are conforming to the Strategic Direction.

The Strategic Direction process analyzes these problem groups and prioritization lists to determine if there is a more general issue affecting the investments. If a general issue is identified, Portfolio Performance may be substantially enhanced by correcting the more general issue. In this manner, several investments may be simultaneously improved by a single corrective action.

Strategic Direction
1. Business Strategy
2. Business Vision
3. System Evaluations
4. System Business Values
1. Strategic Recommendations
1. Issue Identification
2. Corrective Actions
3. Risk Analysis

Figure 24: Strategic Direction process Inputs, Outputs, and Tools & Techniques.

Rationalization Selection
1. Portfolio Valuation
2. Portfolio Performance
3. Business Strategy
4. Business Vision
5. System Evaluations
6. Strategic Alignments
7. Strategic Recommendations
8. System Business Values
1. Rationalization Model
2. Investments for Rationalization
1. Fitness Models
2. Risk Analysis
3. Computational Intelligence
4. Numerical Methods
5. Mathematical Models
6. Requirements Matrices

Figure 25: Rationalization Selection process Inputs, Outputs, and Tools & Techniques.

Best Practice Identification
1. Portfolio Valuation
2. Portfolio Performance
3. Business Strategy
4. Business Vision
5. System Evaluations
6. Strategic Alignments
7. Strategic Recommendations
8. System Business Values
1. Rationalization Model
2. Best Practices
1. Fitness Models
2. Risk Analysis
3. Computational Intelligence
4. Numerical Methods
5. Mathematical Models
6. Requirements Matrices

Figure 26: Best Practice Identification process Inputs, Outputs, and Tools & Techniques.

Transformation
1. Investments for Rationalization
2. Best Practices
3. Business Strategy
4. Business Vision
5. Rationalization Model
1. Transformation Plan
1. Change Recommendations

Figure 27: Transformation process Inputs, Outputs, and Tools & Techniques.

In addition, the Strategic Direction process is dependent on the Prioritization process of the System phase. The Prioritization process results in an investment priority list that is used by the Strategic Direction process to identify the immediate areas for improvement. The assets that have a high priority for rationalization are analyzed first as these investments are predicted to have the most potential for improvement. The prioritization list is the keystone for the efficient and effective administration of the Strategic Direction process.

Finally, the most important input for the Strategic Direction process is the Business Vision. The Business Vision is a document from the business owners specifying how they would like to see the business evolve over time. This statement provides the basis for understanding the overall direction of the organization.

Understanding the direction is essential to the Strategic Direction process because this is an important factor in determining how to evolve the portfolio investments over time. The Business Vision provides the basis for the Strategic Direction process to make recommendations on current and future portfolio investments.

The main result of this process is the Strategic Direction document. This document details recommendations for changes to the portfolio investments in order to achieve the desired Business Vision. These recommendations are directed toward what needs to be done in order to align the portfolio with the Business Vision.

Rationalization Selection
The Rationalization Selection process identifies the particular investments that are targeted for rationalization. This process examines the Portfolio Performance/Valuation, Business Strategy/Vision, Investment Values, and System Evaluations to determine the optimal mix of investments for rationalization.

The Portfolio Performance and Valuation is used to identify particular areas of the portfolio that are performing well and areas that need improvement. This information is combined with the Business Vision and Strategy to evaluate the performance of the portfolio in the light of the business goals and strategy. The Investment Values further identify individual investments that may need rationalization.

All of this information is combined with the System Evaluations to construct the Rationalization Model. These requirement details allow for the specification of requirement matrices. The requirement matrices are used to quickly identify redundancies and gaps in the requirements. Furthermore, the individual requirements may be examined to identify obsolete systems and systems/resources that may be reused.

Finally, based on the portfolio and investment performances, opportunities for investment merger or division may be identified. Some investments may benefit from economies of scale by merging two or more investments into a single system. This is often the case when the investment portfolio is the result of a corporate merger or acquisition. Alternatively, some large investments may benefit by being divided into smaller components. For example, many large projects suffer from a large number of communications lines. If there are isolated components within the project, it may be better to spin the isolated components off into their own independent project to reduce the communication lines and create a more efficient portfolio.

All of this information is combined to create the Rationalization Model. The purpose of this model is to evaluate and select specific investments for rationalization. The Rationalization Model may be a mathematical model, or this may be a manual process of evaluating and selecting appropriate investments. The Rationalization Model is discussed in more detail in Section 9.

Best Practice Identification

Best Practice Identification is in a sense the opposite of Rationalization Selection. In Best Practice Identification, we identify the investments that are performing well and investigate the reasons for their good performance. This information is captured in the Rationalization Model so that it may be applied to other investments in the portfolio during Transformation.

Figure 20 shows an example of Best Practices and Rationalization Targets. Here, investments are values according to 'Number of Users' and 'Cost'. A diagram is created plotting each asset for this two-dimensional valuation. Investments that have high 'Cost' and low 'Number of Users' are targets for rationalization. Alternatively, assets that have a low 'Cost' and a high 'Number of Users' are Best Practices.

Similar to Rationalization Selection, Best Practice Identification examines the Portfolio Performance/Valuation, Business Strategy/Vision, Investment Values, and System Evaluations to determine the investments which are performing well. This information is combined with the System Evaluations to determine the fundamental reasons that underlie their performance.

Understanding the reasons for the better performance of these investments leads to identification of organizational Best Practices. The Best Practices may align with Best Practices recognized in the industry. In this case, guidance from industry standards may be used to further improve the performance.

Alternatively, the identified Best Practices may be unique to the organization. In this case, it is important to conduct a detailed examination to identify why these investments work so well within the organization. These practices are of particular importance as they may not be generally known to the Investment Owners or other Rationalization Managers within the organization. Documenting these practices and disseminating the information throughout the organization may lead to enhanced performance across the entire business.

These Best Practices are also incorporated into the Rationalization Model. By incorporating this information, the Rationalization Model can identify investments that represent the portfolio ideal and direct the rationalization effort to enhancing other investments by incorporating Best Practices.

Transformation

The Transformation process documents specific actions that should be performed to affect the Strategic Direction Document. The Transformation is an action plan detailing specific actions that need to be carried out in order to move the portfolio from its current state to the desired future state.

The Transformation process depends on both the Strategic Alignment and Strategic Direction processes. The Strategic Alignment documents where the portfolio currently stands, whereas the Strategic Direction process determines where it needs to go. The Transformation process is used to figure out how we get from here to there.

The Transformation process also depends on the Rationalization Selection and Best Practice Identification processes. These processes identify the investments that need rationalization as well as the organizational Best Practices. The Best Practices may be applied to the Rationalization Targets to improve their performance.

The main output of the Transformation process is the Transformation Plan. The Transformation Plan is a document providing details on what steps need to be taken in order to achieve the desired goals. This document is the main output of portfolio rationalization and provides the fundamental rationale for making changes to the portfolio investments.

Review

This section lists the major activities that make up the Portfolio Rationalization Process. These major activities provide the base elements required for portfolio rationalization.

Essentially, investment data is acquired (Portfolio Snapshot), a valuation scheme is identified (Business Value Definition), the investments are valued (Investment Valuation), requirements are considered (System Evaluation), the current state is evaluated (Strategic Alignment), the desired future state is considered (Strategic Direction), and a plan is presented to move us in the right direction (Transformation).

A specific Portfolio Rationalization Process will tailor these activities to create a well-defined process. Which activities are used and how much emphasis is placed on this is determined by the Rationalization Manager.

4 Process Dependencies and Life Cycle

The previous section discussed the activities of portfolio rationalization. These activities are interdependent because inputs to some processes are the outputs from other processes. This section examines the dependencies between the processes and presents the Portfolio Rationalization Lifecycle.

The Portfolio Rationalization Lifecycle provides the ability for the processes to update based on input from any other process. The dependencies as listed should be interpreted as a requirement to begin a process. For example, the Category Definition process cannot be initiated the first time until the Portfolio Snapshot process is complete.

Once these processes are each initialized, they may continue to operate without requiring a dependent process to be executed. For instance, once the entire process has initiated, we may find that we would like to include an additional category as part of the Investment Categories. In this case, we can update the Category Definition process without first updating the Portfolio Snapshot. Once the Category Definition is rerun, we can continue to execute the remaining processes and eventually obtain an updated Transformation Plan even though we never reran the Portfolio Snapshot.

In this respect the processes may be considered to be running independently and parallel to one another. This is useful as portfolio rationalization should be considered a continuous, ongoing process rather than a one-time project.

Furthermore, the processes do not need to run in a strictly linear fashion. The processes may run continually and even incorporate feedback from downstream processes. For example, the Portfolio Valuation process may identify the need for a new category and notify the Category Definition process to update.

In this case, the Portfolio Valuation process may choose to wait until this update is processed through the entire stream of rationalization. Alternatively, the Portfolio Valuation process may finish executing and proceed to the next steps, and allow the new category to take effect in future executions of the rationalization process.

The life cycle for portfolio rationalization is an initiation phase followed by an auto-iterative cycle. After the rationalization process is initially executed, the auto-iterative cycle takes over and each of the processes can be triggered by the results of any other process. Thus, the final output of portfolio rationalization may prompt an update to the Investment Categories, Business Value Definition, Cluster Modeling, etc.

If an update is indicated, the governing process is rerun incorporating the updated information. This may be modifying an Investment Category, a Numerical Method, or the process itself. In any case, once the governing process is rerun, the processes that follow in the dependency chain are also rerun. This eventually terminates in a new, updated Transformation Plan.

Input-Output Flow

Figure 28 diagrams the flow of process inputs and outputs. Inputs and outputs are displayed as hexagons, while processes are shown as squares. Light hexagons indicate inputs external to the Portfolio Rationalization Process, while the dark hexagons indicate inputs and outputs that are generated by Portfolio Rationalization Processes.

Figure 28 indicates a linear process starting from the Portfolio Snapshot, continuing through various processes, and ending with the Transformation Plan.

However, the portfolio rationalization life cycle is not a strictly linear process. Each of these processes may run continuously and independently. In addition, downstream processes may provide feedback to upstream processes. In this sense, the portfolio rationalization life cycle is a continuous activity that feeds back on itself.

Any process on the chain may prompt an update for a different process. This will start a new cycle of updates to the processes as each dependent process is rerun. If the process is an upstream process, this may cause a temporary halt as previous processes are updated and rerun. Alternatively, execution may continue while the upstream process is updated.

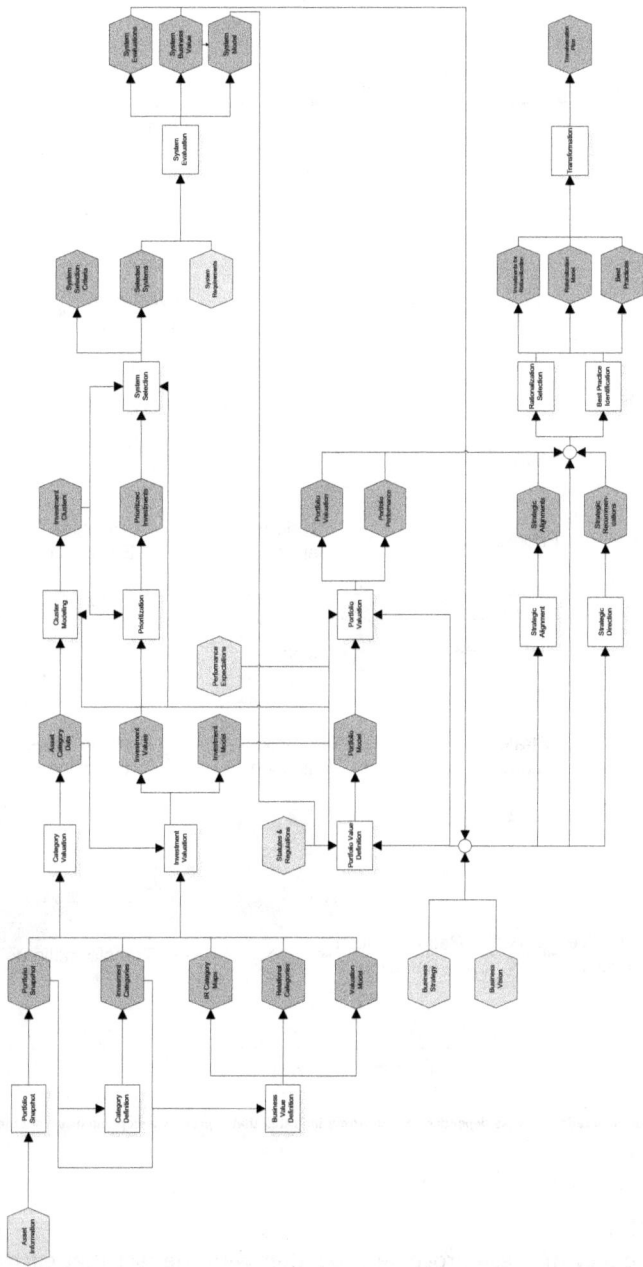

Figure 28: Inputs, Outputs, and Process flow for portfolio rationalization.

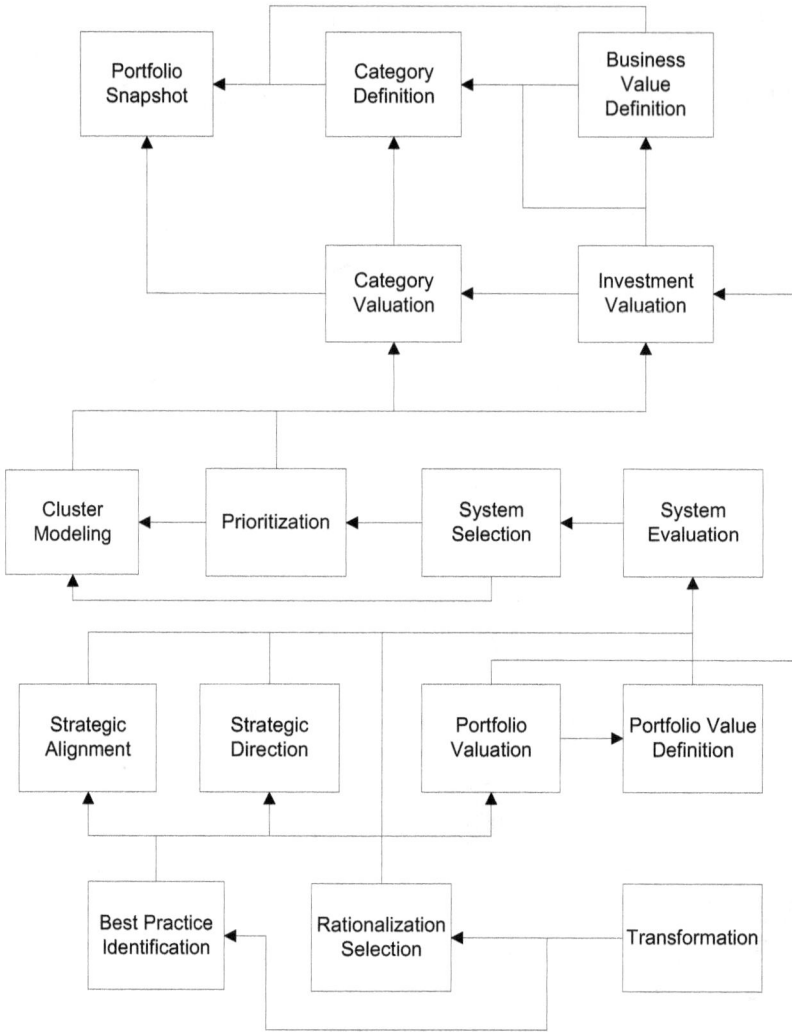

Figure 29: Portfolio rationalization process dependencies. An arrow indicates that a process is dependent on another process.

Dependencies

The interdependency of these processes, together with the fact that each process may run independently and concurrently with the others, make the entire portfolio rationalization lifecycle a dynamic recurrent network. The network is dynamic because each of the processes is able to update and modify the portfolio rationalization process. In addition, the network is recurrent because the processes are interconnected with processes feeding information to each other, making recurrent network connections.

This dynamic recurrent network structure allows the Portfolio Rationalization Process the ability to demonstrate Computational Intelligence as the entire process may be constructed to adapt to new information and situations as more information becomes available.

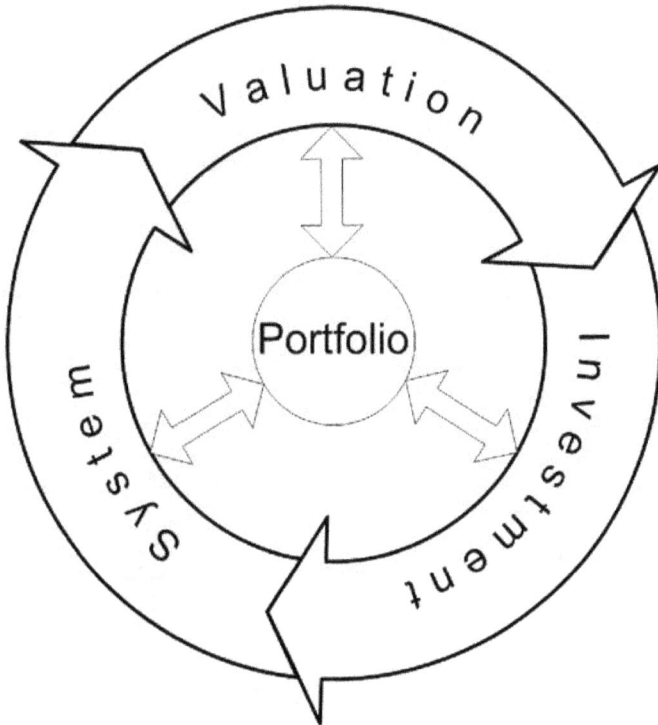

Figure 30: The Portfolio Rationalization Lifecycle.

Furthermore, the entire process may be rerun based on updating the Portfolio Snapshot. However, it may not be necessary to rerun all of the processes. For instance, the Category Definition process may not need to be rerun unless there is a reason to review the Investment Categories. If there is no need to review these categories, this process may be skipped. Similarly, the Business Valuation Definition may also be skipped if there is no need to reconsider the Investment Models already in place.

Portfolio Rationalization Lifecycle
Figure 30 is a graphical representation of the portfolio rationalization life cycle. This diagram shows the Valuation, Investment, and System phases working in a cycle, while each of these phases feeds the Portfolio phase. Furthermore, the results of the Portfolio phase can feed and update each

of the other phases, restarting the cycle. This auto-iterative life cycle provides flexibility to the portfolio rationalization methodology, allowing it to adjust to new situations and the unexpected results which often occur as the Business Strategy and Vision change.

5 Valuation Model

The Valuation Model is used to identify categories that may be useful in assessing business value. The Valuation Model examines the raw data available for the portfolio investments and determines which data has sufficient quality to be useful in computing business value.

The Valuation Model does not compute the business value for the investments. The Investment Model is responsible for assigning business value to each investment. The Valuation Model identifies the categories that may be used as a basis for the business value. The Investment Model digests this category information and uses this to formulate business value for the investments.

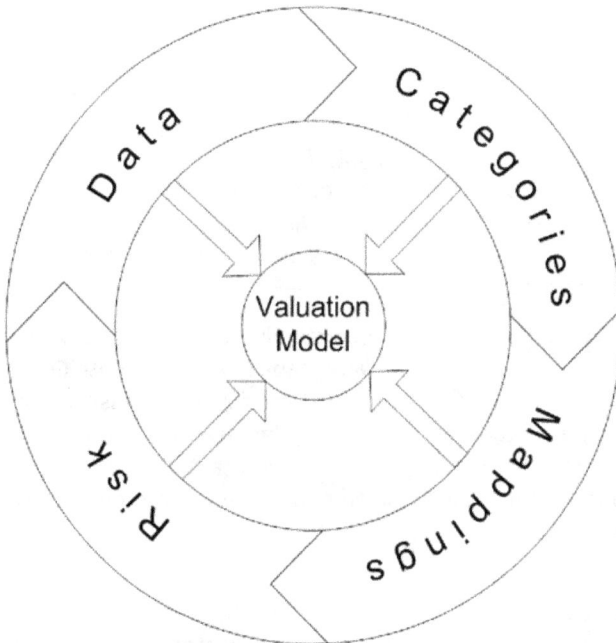

Figure 31: The Valuation Model is based on factors such as Quality, Risk, Impact, Capability, and Maturity.

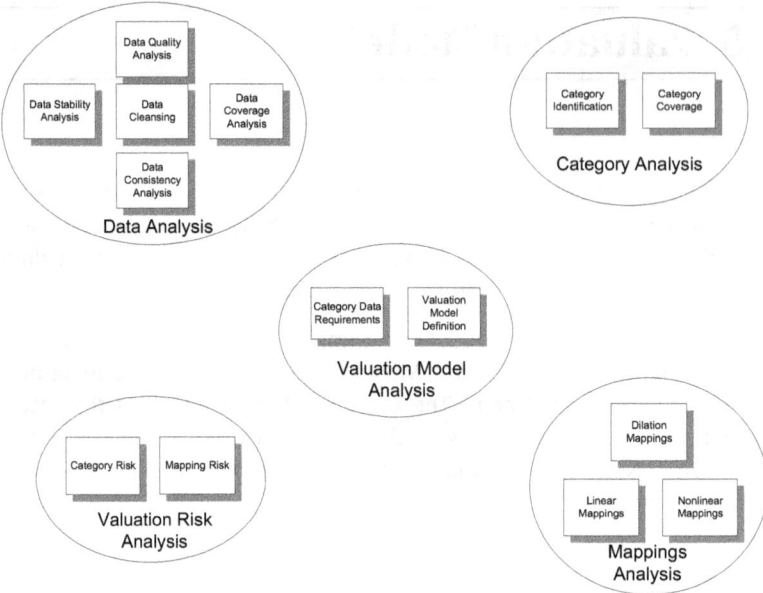

Figure 32: The Valuation Model process.

Data Analysis

The Data Analysis category is primarily concerned with measuring the quality of the data used to create the Portfolio Snapshot. This is perhaps the most important and often the most overlooked aspect of Investment Modeling. In the end, the utility of the values computed by the model are only as good as the data provided.

The Data Analysis category is divided into five sub-areas: Data Quality Analysis, Data Consistency Analysis, Data Stability Analysis, Data Coverage Analysis, and Data Cleansing. The first of these five sub-areas contributes to the uncertainty of the value computed by the model. As discussed earlier, the uncertainty in the value is as important as the value itself. Without a proper estimate of the uncertainty, the value produced by the model is useless.

The Data Quality Analysis sub-area focuses on measuring how well the data gathered conforms to requirements. If the data does not have sufficient coverage, or if the type of data is unexpected, the data may not be useful for the model.

Data Quality Analysis
1. Portfolio Snapshot
1. Data Quality Standard
2. Data Quality Document
1. Statistical Techniques
2. Mathematical Models
3. Numerical Methods

Data Consistency Analysis
1. Portfolio Snapshot
1. Data Consistency Document
1. Statistical Techniques
2. Mathematical Models
3. Numerical Methods

Data Stability Analysis
1. Portfolio Snapshot
1. Data Stability Document
1. Statistical Techniques
2. Mathematical Models
3. Numerical Methods

Figure 33: Data Quality Analysis process Inputs, Outputs, and Tools & Techniques.

Figure 34: Data Consistency Analysis process Inputs, Outputs, and Tools & Techniques.

Figure 35: Data Stability Analysis process Inputs, Outputs, and Tools & Techniques.

Data Coverage Analysis
1. Portfolio Snapshot
1. Data Coverage Document
1. Statistical Techniques

Data Cleansing
1. Portfolio Snapshot
2. Data Quality Document
3. Data Consistency Document
4. Data Stability Document
5. Data Coverage Document
1. Updated Portfolio Snapshot
1. Statistical Techniques
2. Mathematical Models
3. Numerical Methods

Figure 36: Data Coverage Analysis process Inputs, Outputs, and Tools & Techniques.

Figure 37: Data Cleansing process Inputs, Outputs, and Tools & Techniques.

Data Stability Analysis evaluates the frequency and amount of change to the data over time. Data that changes rapidly and over wide ranges is less reliable than data that is slowly varying. As such, the uncertainty associated with this data is larger and should be reflected in the Investment Model.

The Data Consistency Analysis sub-area addresses questions about the consistency of the data when different measurements are made. For example, a specific data field may be measured in different ways. If more than one method is used, we may end up with different values for the field depending on which measurement we look at. Problems such as this also contribute to the uncertainty of the model value.

Data Coverage Analysis examines the field-level coverage of the data. This information is essential in identifying data fields that can be used to compare investments. Fields with low Data Coverage have a narrow use for comparing investments. However, these can be useful when analyzing a highly specific group of investments. Alternatively, fields with high Data Coverage may present opportunities to compare a wide range of investments.

Data Cleansing corrects faulty data. This process uses the results of Data Quality analysis to identify problematic data elements and attempts to make corrections where possible. This leads to a more consistent data set which in turn leads to better rationalization results. These processes provide inputs to the Data Cleansing process. Data Cleansing reviews the data and transforms it to correct inconsistent and inaccurate information from the snapshot. Faulty data can lead to incorrect valuation of the investment or even incorrect rationalization decisions. This process identifies faulty data and corrects it to the extent possible.

Data Quality Analysis

The Data Quality Analysis sub-area is a quantitative quality control process with respect to the Portfolio Snapshot. After an initial Portfolio Snapshot is obtained, the data is examined and a set of quality standards is constructed. This initial information is used to specify the data quality standard that is expected for future Portfolio Snapshots.

The Data Quality Standard is a document specifying what fields are present in the Portfolio Snapshot, the data type of each field, and a minimum coverage. Each individual specification as to the nature of a part of the Portfolio Snapshot is called a Quality Rule.

A checklist is created with an entry for every Quality Rule. Every time a new Portfolio Snapshot is created, a Data Quality Analysis is performed and a quality checklist is completed. The completed checklist evaluates every Quality Rule and documents whether the snapshot obeys the rule.

The checklist may be computed automatically via a computer program. Many of the rules in a checklist can be evaluated by software tools. In these cases, it may be efficient to automatically compute a checklist every time a new snapshot is compiled. A compliance report may be prepared as new checklists are compiled.

Data Quality Analysis examines several aspects of the data to determine the overall quality. The list below details some of the more common elements that are reviewed:

Correctness - Evaluates whether the data in the snapshot is correct. The Portfolio Rationalization Process fundamentally relies on the information in the Portfolio Snapshot. If this data is incorrect, the rationalization decisions may be incorrect.

Accuracy – Examines groups of data elements to verify that they are correct in combination. For example, if a recordset has a zip code and a city name, accuracy evaluates if the zip code is correct for the city.

Integrity – Datasets in relational databases often have keys referring to records in other tables. Integrity verifies that these referred records are in fact present. If the data does not have integrity, then all of the necessary information may not be present for proper analysis.

Completeness – Determines if groups of fields are presented together when required. Some fields require that other fields have defined values. If these other values are not specified, we can end up with inconsistent results.

Validity – Examines the data to assure that every field has a valid value. Invalid values can lead to unpredictable results because these values were not anticipated when defining the methods of computing Business Value.

Consistency – Identifies inconsistent data in the data set. This typically requires some set of predetermined rules in order to effectively identify inconsistent data. Inconsistent data can lead to inconsistent analysis results and should be corrected whenever possible.[48]

Coverage - Data Coverage is the percent of data present for a given field. Data Coverage is useful in determining which fields present opportunities to relatively compare investments. Two investments may be compared when both a value present for the same field[49]

Uniqueness – Examines the data set to identify duplicate records in the data. Duplicate records cause problems because statistical analysis of the data counts the individual records without understanding that some are duplicates. This biases the results and can lead to rationalization errors.

Data Stability Analysis

Data Stability Analysis compares successive Portfolio Snapshots taken over time to estimate the extent and variance of the data. The data changes may be evaluated over the entire dataset, for a field over the dataset, for a particular investment, or for a field for each investment. Data Stability Analysis is the statistical variation of the data values over time.

The first step is to quantify the changes to a field. The quantification should account for the difference between the old value and new value. If the data is a numeric field, this may simply be the difference. If the field is character based, an appropriate measure should be constructed depending on the information in the field. At a minimum, we may simply take a Boolean value of 0 to indicate no change or 1 to indicate that the data has been modified.

---

[48] Note that consistency is handled as a separate process in Data Consistency Analysis. A separate process is used because the Portfolio Snapshot is often compiled from a variety of data sources, and data consistency and the means to deal with inconsistent data are a common problem.

[49] Similar to consistency, Data Coverage is also handled as a separate process. Difficulties with Data Coverage have a significant impact on the ability to formulate Business Values and are handled as a distinct process.

If the degree of variance can be computed, we can use this as the measure of uncertainty of the value of each data field. In this respect, every field f can be associated with an error Δf. When we use the field data in formulas, we can propagate the error through standard error propagation analysis. Specifically, if we have $f \pm \Delta f$ and some function $g(x)$, then

$$\Delta g^2 = \left(\frac{\partial f}{\partial x}\right)^2 (\Delta x)^2. \qquad \text{5-1}$$

Data Consistency Analysis

Data Consistency Analysis compares two different measurements of the same data field. For example, we may obtain a value for the field via interview, and get another value from a questionnaire. These values can be different, and this difference can be statistically analyzed. Data Consistency Analysis measures the statistical variation of the measurement of the field value.

Data Consistency Analysis faces similar challenges as Data Stability Analysis, and similar techniques may be employed. We need to quantify the variance of the different measurements, and this can be done in a variety of ways depending on the underlying data type.

Data consistency is also addressed during Data Quality Analysis. However, data consistency is a common problem in portfolio rationalization. Because of this, this particular element is defined as a separate process.

Data Coverage Analysis

Data Coverage is a measure of the percent of investments that have useful information for a specific data field. In particular, if there are n total investments in the portfolio and d of these have data available for this field, the Data Coverage is

$$C = d/n. \qquad \text{5-2}$$

As an example, assume there are 100 investments in the portfolio. Let 'Number of Users' be one of the fields. If only 80 of the investments have a value for this field, then the Data Coverage for this field is

$$C = \frac{80}{100} = 0.80 = 80\%. \qquad \text{5-3}$$

The Data Coverage is a measure of how useful a particular data field is for evaluating investments. Fields that have low Data Coverage have a more narrow use than fields with a high Data Coverage. The Category Definition process accounts for this information when choosing categories.

Data Coverage also examines the variance in the field data. A field may have coverage of 100%, but this is useless as a comparator if every investment has the same value for the field.

Data Coverage computes how many different values are present. This may be computed by taking the total number of distinct values and dividing by the total number of investments, or by examining the standard deviation.

Data Coverage is also addressed in Data Quality Analysis. Similar to Data Consistency Analysis, Data Coverage is particularly important in portfolio rationalization, so it is defined as a distinct process.

Data Cleansing

The Data Cleansing process aims to identify and/or correct faulty data in the Portfolio Snapshot. The process examines the Data Coverage, Data Quality Analysis, Data Consistency Analysis, and Data Stability Analysis to assess several aspects of the data.

These factors are analyzed to determine the overall quality of the data. Deficiencies are marked and corrected if possible. The deficiencies should be noted and accounted for in the Business Valuation Model.

Category Analysis

Category Analysis analyzes the available raw data and determines which categories are suitable for used in computing business value. The purpose is not to identify which categories are important measures of value. Instead, these processes examine the quality of the underlying data set minimum quality standards for the data. Datasets that do not meet the minimum quality standards are discarded as unreliable.

Category Identification
1. Portfolio Snapshot
2. Investment Categories
1. IR Category Maps
2. Relational Categories
1. Data Analysis

Category Coverage
1. Portfolio Snapshot
2. Investment Categories
3. Relational Categories
4. IR Category Maps
1. Asset Category Coverage
1. Data Analysis

Figure 38: Category Identification process Inputs, Outputs, and Tools & Techniques.

Figure 39: Category Coverage process Inputs, Outputs, and Tools & Techniques.

Category Identification

Category Identification examines the raw data and relates the various data categories. This analysis is done using the Portfolio Snapshot and Investment Categories.

This process is different in purpose from the Category Definition process. The Category Definition process aims to identify all available categories. Category Identification examines the list of all available categories, determines how the categories relate, normalizes the information, and compiles the information together into a list of Relational Categories.

In a sense, the Relational Categories form a database schema for the category information. In addition, this process identifies the IR Category Maps. These maps identify which raw categories (from the Investment Categories list) map to the Relational Categories.

Individual Investment Categories may be combined together, dissected, or parsed to form individual Relational Categories. For example, we may have a 'Point of Contact' field for 'IT Hardware' and a different 'Point of Contact' field for 'IT Software'. Each of these 'Point of Contact' fields may be an Investment Category. Here, we may decide to combine these two sets of data into a single 'Point of Contact' field and setup relations between this final dataset and the 'IT Hardware' and 'IT Software' categories.

At this stage, we are only concerned with identifying the relationships in the Relational Categories. The Mapping Analysis that follows identifies specific mappings from the Investment Categories to the Relational Categories.

Category Coverage

Category Coverage is a standard data coverage analysis applied to the Relational Categories. This process identifies the field-level coverage of the Relational Categories which is used during Investment Model Analysis to assist with the specification of the Investment Model.

The output of Category Coverage is the Asset Category Coverage. This document computes the coverage for both the Investment and Relational Categories. The Asset Category Coverage is used during the Category Data Requirements process to assist in the specification of the Category Quality Standard as well as identifying the Passed Relational Categories.

Mappings Analysis

Mappings Analysis examines potential mappings between Relational Categories to formulate business value. The analysis is broken into Dilation Mappings, Linear Mappings, Nonlinear Mappings. These are handled separately because the Dilation Mappings are very common, Linear Mappings are typically common, and the Nonlinear Mappings are typically more complex.

Dilation Mappings
1. Portfolio Snapshot
2. Investment Categories
1. IR Category Maps
2. Relational Categories
1. Data Analysis

Linear Mappings
1. Portfolio Snapshot
2. Investment Categories
1. IR Category Maps
2. Relational Categories
1. Data Analysis

Nonlinear Mappings
1. Portfolio Snapshot
2. Investment Categories
1. IR Category Maps
2. Relational Categories
1. Data Analysis

Figure 40: Dilation Mappings process Inputs, Outputs, and Tools & Techniques.

Figure 41: Linear Mappings process Inputs, Outputs, and Tools & Techniques.

Figure 42: Nonlinear Mappings process Inputs, Outputs, and Tools & Techniques.

Dilation Mappings

Dilation Mappings are simple scaling and translations of the Investment Categories. For example, we may have an Investment Category for 'Employee Satisfaction' taken from a survey. The raw data is on the range from 0 to 5. We desire a Relational Category on the range from 1 to 10. Let I be the Investment Category data and R be the Relational Category data. The dilation transformation relating these is

$$R = \frac{9}{5}I + 1$$

Dilation Mappings are linear transformations that only involve a single Investment Category.

Linear Mappings

Linear Mappings are mappings of Investment Categories to Relational Categories that are linear transformations but involve more than one category. For example, suppose we have two employee satisfactions surveys taken six months apart. Each of these surveys is an independent Investment Category. We may want to compute a Relational Category that is the average of the two:

$$R = \frac{I_1 + I_2}{2}$$

Nonlinear Mappings

Nonlinear Mappings are mappings of Investment Categories in a nonlinear way. For example, if an investment has a category for 'Number of Users' and another category for 'Cost', we may want to compute the 'Cost per User' Relational Category as:

$$R = \frac{N}{C}$$

Alternatively, we may have data that covers a wide range and wish to scale this according to standard data analysis techniques. For example, we may have an Investment Category with a field of 'User Clicks'. Because some applications may have only a few clicks per month while others have several clicks per second, the data in this category may vary over a wide range. To scale this, we may wish to examine the natural logarithm of the Investment Category:

$$R = \ln Clicks$$

This is also a nonlinear map. Although the map only involves one Investment Category, this is not a Dilation Mapping because the transformation is nonlinear.

Valuation Risk Analysis

Valuation Risk Analysis examines the uncertainties in the Relational Categories due to inherent uncertainties in the data as well as uncertainties from the mappings that produce the Relational Categories.

Category Risk
1. Portfolio Snapshot 2. Investment Categories
1. Category Risk Assessment
1. Data Analysis

Mapping Risk
1. Portfolio Snapshot 2. Investment Categories 3. Relational Categories 4. IR Category Maps 5. Category Risk Assessment
1. Mapping Risk Assessment
1. Data Analysis

Figure 43: Category Risk process Inputs, Outputs, and Tools & Techniques.

Figure 44: Mapping Risk process Inputs, Outputs, and Tools & Techniques.

Category Risk

Category Risk is the uncertainty in the Investment Category values due to uncertainties in the raw data. This risk quantifies the measurement uncertainty in the data.

There is always some uncertainty in the measured value. Even when a category is as simple as a yes/no field, there is still some uncertainty associated with the value. For example, some of the data may be incorrect because of typographical errors during data entry, corruption during data transmission, or misunderstanding on the part of the evaluator. In any case, there will be some finite, non-zero uncertainty associated with every Relational and Investment Category.

The output of Category Risk is the Category Risk Assessment. This document specifies the uncertainty associated with each Investment Category. These uncertainties provide the basis for computing the Relational Category uncertainties in the Mapping Risk process.

Mapping Risk

Mapping Risk is the uncertainty in the Relational Category value arising from the mapping between the Investment Categories and the Relational Category. This uncertainty may be computed using standard error propagation techniques.

To compute the Mapping Risk, we begin with the Category Risk Assessment from the Category Risk process and the IR Category Maps from the Mapping Analysis. We apply error propagation to the IR Category Maps to determine the formulae for expressing the uncertainties in the Relational Categories. We can evaluate these expressions using the Category Risk Assessment, Investment Categories, and the Portfolio Snapshot.

Valuation Model Analysis

Valuation Model Analysis compiles the results from the previous processes to formulate the Valuation Model. The Valuation Model is the mathematical method used to specify the valuation of the Relational and Investment Categories.

Category Data Requirements
1. Portfolio Snapshot
2. Investment Categories
3. Relational Categories
4. Category Risk Assessment
5. Mapping Risk Assessment
6. Data Quality Standard
7. Data Quality Document
8. Data Consistency Document
9. Data Stability Document
10. Data Coverage Document
11. Asset Category Coverage
1. Category Quality Standard
2. Passed Relational Categories
1. Data Analysis

Figure 45: Category Data Requirements process Inputs, Outputs, and Tools & Techniques.

Valuation Model Definition
1. Passed Relational Categories
2. Mapping Risk Assessment
3. Investment Categories
4. Relational Categories
5. IR Category Maps
1. Valuation Model
1. Data Analysis

Figure 46: Valuation Model Definition process Inputs, Outputs, and Tools & Techniques.

Category Data Requirements

Category Data Requirements are minimal quality requirements that must be met in order to consider an Investment or Relational Category as having sufficient quality for consideration. Categories that do not meet this minimum threshold should be discarded and not used for computing business value.

This process outputs the Category Quality Standard and the Passed Relational Categories. The Category Quality Standard is a document specifying the quality standard for the Relational Categories. This quality standard is applied to the Relational Categories to determine the set of Passed Relational Categories. These are the categories that are determined to be sufficient to pass the Category Quality Standard.

Valuation Model Definition

Value Model Definition specifies the mathematical model used to compute the values associated with the Investment and Relational Categories. This process produces the Valuation Model which is one of the critical portfolio rationalization models.

This process examines the results of Data Analysis, Category Analysis, Mappings Analysis, and Valuation Risk Analysis to produce a mathematical specification of how values are constructed from the field data in the Investment and Relational Categories. The Valuation Model is used by the Investment Phase in order to assign values to the categories and to compute the business value for the investments.

6 Investment Model

The Investment Model is the means used to assign Business Value to each of the portfolio investments. This model is a key aspect of Portfolio Rationalization. The model should incorporate the essential factors that make the investment important to the organization, but not contain so much information as to become overburdened and overly complex. In addition, the model should identify values that are comparable between significant numbers of investments.

Assessing business value is a key element to portfolio rationalization. Business value can be difficult to determine for non-financial assets. This section reviews some of the factors that may be considered when assessing business value. Specific factors presented here may not be important for some investments, and it is anticipated that a given portfolio may not use all of the factors listed here.

Similarly, these factors are not intended to be an exhaustive list. There are a wide variety of non-financial investments that may be considered under a portfolio rationalization operation. Certain investments may lend themselves to additional factors not presented here. Again, any particular rationalization operation should tailor the valuation process to the investments in the portfolio at hand.

In general, we classify the Investment Model analysis into six categories: Quality Analysis Investment Risk Analysis, Impact Analysis, Capability Analysis, Maturity Analysis, and Investment Model Analysis. Each of these five categories has sub-areas that should be considered when modeling business value. Figure 48 shows the categories in relation to the Investment phase of the portfolio rationalization life cycle. We see that each of these categories contributes to the Investment Model for the Business Value.

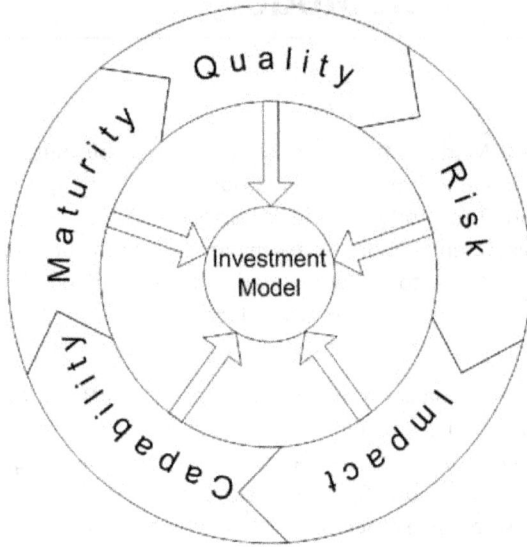

Figure 47: The Investment Model is based on factors such as Risk, Impact, Capability, and Maturity.

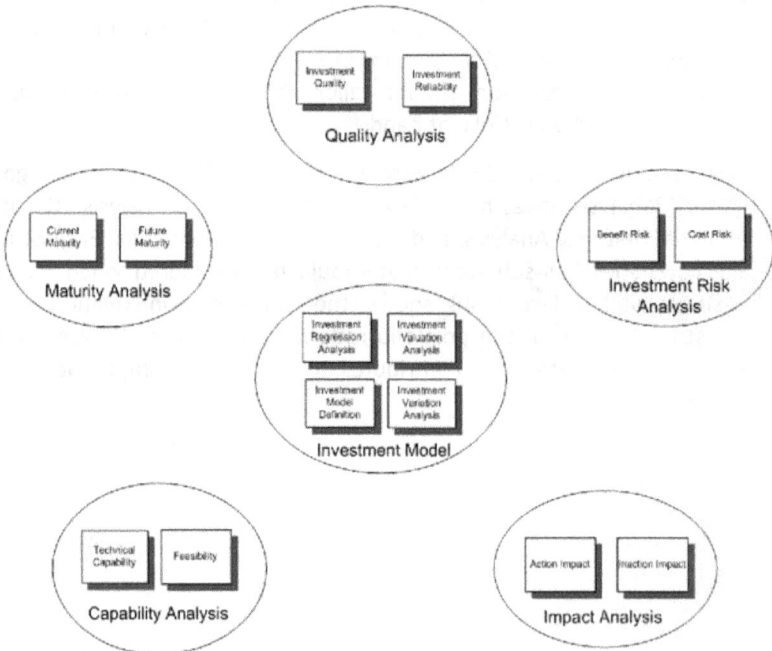

Figure 48: The Investment Model process.

Quality Analysis

Quality Analysis examines the quality and reliability of the investment as a whole. These processes are applied to the actual investment, not the underlying data as per the Data Analysis processes from the Valuation phase.

Investment Quality determines how well the investment conforms to expectations while Investment Reliability measured how consistently the investment performs. These measures are similar to the measurements of precision and accuracy in data analysis.

Investment Quality
1. Portfolio Snapshot
2. Data Quality Document
3. Data Stability Document
4. Data Consistency Document
1. Investment Quality Document
1. Risk Analysis

Figure 49: Investment Quality process Inputs, Outputs, and Tools & Techniques.

Investment Reliability
1. Portfolio Snapshot
2. Data Quality Document
3. Data Stability Document
4. Data Consistency Document
1. Investment Reliability Document
1. Risk Analysis

Figure 50: Investment Reliability process Inputs, Outputs, and Tools & Techniques.

Investment Quality

Investment Quality is a measure of how well the investment meets expectations. The expectations may be conformance to a set of system requirements, a return on investment, or other such performance measure.

The Investment Model may use this information when assigning business value to the investment. Investments which are not close to meeting expectations may be valued lower than investments that are conforming.

Investment Reliability

Investment Reliability measures how consistent the investment performs over a series of measurements. This is analogous to measurements of accuracy in data analysis.

The Investment Model may use Investment Reliability as a factor in determining the business value for the investment. For example, an investment that is consistently producing the same performance may be valued even though the performance does not meet expectations. In some case, consistency in performance may be a value into itself.

Investment Risk Analysis

The area of risk analysis is well developed and many standard techniques can be applied in the analysis of the field data. We will not endeavor to summarize all of the methods of Risk Analysis. However, we will examine two simplified risk areas: Benefit Risk and Cost Risk.

The Benefit Risk is the uncertainty in the valuation of the asset benefit, while the Cost Risk is the uncertainty in the valuation of the asset cost. Both of these variances can be useful in computing the variance of the Investment Valuation.

Benefit Risk
1. Portfolio Snapshot
2. Data Quality Document
3. Data Stability Document
4. Data Consistency Document
1. Benefit Risk Document
1. Risk Analysis

Cost Risk
1. Portfolio Snapshot
2. Data Quality Document
3. Data Stability Document
4. Data Consistency Document
1. Cost Risk Document
1. Risk Analysis

Figure 51: Benefit Risk process Inputs, Outputs, and Tools & Techniques.

Figure 52: Cost Risk process Inputs, Outputs, and Tools & Techniques.

Benefit Risk

The Benefit Risk is a measure of the uncertainty of the value of the benefit of the investment. In many non-financial investments, it is common to ignore this uncertainty and assume it is zero. However, if a variance is available, it may be used to further estimate the uncertainty in the underlying investment value.

The Benefit Risk is one contributor to the overall uncertainty in the value of an investment. This error should be quantified as some ΔV against an investment with value V. This error may be combined with other risk errors to formulate an overall uncertainty in the investment value.

Cost Risk

Cost Risk is similar to Benefit Risk, except the uncertainty is in the investment cost rather than in the benefit. Again, many non-financial investments ignore the Cost Risk and assume that it is zero. However, if a Cost Risk is available, it should be used to assist with the computation of the uncertainty in the Investment Valuation.

The Cost Risk is another contributor to the overall uncertainty in the value of an investment. Similar to the Benefit Risk, the error associated with the Cost Risk should be quantified as some ΔV against an investment with value V. This error may be combined with other risk errors to formulate an overall uncertainty in the investment value.

Impact Analysis

Impact Analysis quantifies the impact the investment has on the overall portfolio, and what impact changes the investment may have. Some investments may be underperforming, but may present a desirable diversification of assets. Eliminating these assets may at first appear to be warranted, but removal of these assets can lead to a less stable portfolio.

Impact Analysis examines both the impact of taking action and not taking action with the investment. In this respect, a value may be computed to associate with each of these possibilities, and these values can assist in determining if the investment should be modified.

Action Impact
1. Portfolio Snapshot
1. Action Impact Document
1. Risk Analysis

Figure 53: Action Impact process Inputs, Outputs, and Tools & Techniques.

Inaction Impact
1. Portfolio Snapshot
1. Inaction Impact Document
1. Risk Analysis

Figure 54: Inaction Impact process Inputs, Outputs, and Tools & Techniques.

Action Impact

The Action Impact attempts to quantify how a specific investment action may affect the Investment Value, Portfolio Value, investment uncertainty, and portfolio uncertainty. In addition, the Action Impact may be used to examine the impact to Investment Clusters or other aspects of the portfolio.

Inaction Impact

The Inaction Impact is similar to the Action Impact, except (of course) that this time we make a quantitative estimate of what we may gain or lose by not taking action. This is in part a measure of opportunity cost for the particular investment action in question.

Capability Analysis

Capability Analysis quantifies the overall capability of an investment. Some investments can be measured according to their ability to deliver a useful result. This analysis attempts to quantify this concept and use it to update the Investment Value.

For example, we may have a portfolio containing two different word processing applications. By itself, this seems like a waste of resources because economies of scale are not maximized. However, it may be the case that one application is generally useful and inexpensive, while the other application is used to produce highly specialized marketing materials. It may be better to keep both applications rather than eliminating one. Capability Analysis attempts to capture and quantify these situations.

Technical Capability
1. Portfolio Snapshot
1. Technical Capability Document
1. Requirements Analysis

Figure 55: Technical Capability process Inputs, Outputs, and Tools & Techniques.

Feasibility
1. Portfolio Snapshot
1. Feasibility Document
1. Requirements Analysis

Figure 56: Feasibility process Inputs, Outputs, and Tools & Techniques.

Technical Capability

Technical Capability examines the technical aspects of the investment capability. There may not be an easy way to quantify Technical Capability. Nonetheless, creating some measure can be beneficial. Even a basic model will allow Investment Valuations the flexibility to reach situations like the example above.

However, when there is no easy method to quantify Technical Capability, we need to be careful not to use this to arbitrarily modify the portfolio rationalization results. Subjective valuations of Technical Capability can lead to abusive manipulation of the results to favor or disfavor a specific investment.

Feasibility

While Technical Capability measures the current capability of an asset, Feasibility measures the future capability of the investment. Feasibility has the same drawbacks and problems as Technical Capability. However, Feasibility has the added element that the future capability is even more difficult to quantify than present capability.

Maturity Analysis

Maturity Analysis quantifies an investment's level of maturity. Many non-financial investments move through various phases over the life cycle of the asset. This analysis attempts to measure and incorporate this information into the Investment Model.

Current Maturity
1. Portfolio Snapshot
1. Current Maturity Document
1. Requirements Analysis

Figure 57: Current Maturity process Inputs, Outputs, and Tools & Techniques.

Future Maturity
1. Portfolio Snapshot
1. Future Maturity Document
1. Requirements Analysis

Figure 58: Future Maturity process Inputs, Outputs, and Tools & Techniques.

Current Maturity

The Current Maturity measures the current maturity state of the asset and incorporates this information into the Investment Model. Quantifying Current Maturity faces many of the same challenges as quantifying Technical Capability and Feasibility. As such, care should be taken to not misuse this field to direct the portfolio by hand.

Future Maturity

The Future Maturity measures the future maturity state of the asset and incorporates this information into the Investment Model. This process is similar to quantifying Current Maturity and faces many of the same challenges. However, just as with Feasibility, Future Maturity is even less certain than present maturity.

Model Analysis

Model Analysis is the determination and specification of a particular model or models to assess the Business Value of an investment based on the data fields available and the other factors analyzed in this section. The main purpose of the model is to create one or more values that allow different assets to be compared. This model is one of the most fundamental items used in portfolio rationalization.

The model should be tailored for each specific portfolio. Different portfolios require different valuation of the investments. As such, two different portfolios may have vastly different models even though they have similar investments. The different models reflect differing concerns between portfolios.

We should be careful to understand that because models may be different between portfolios, we cannot compare the Business Value for assets between portfolios. Although both models may produce similar numeric values, since the method of computing the values is different, the values are not comparable.

Investment Regression Analysis
1. Portfolio Snapshot
2. Benefit Risk Document
3. Cost Risk Document
1. Investment Regression Document
1. Statistical Techniques
2. Mathematical Models
3. Numerical Methods

Investment Valuation Analysis
1. Portfolio Snapshot
2. Benefit Risk Document
3. Cost Risk Document
4. Investment Regression Document
1. Investment Valuation Document
1. Statistical Techniques
2. Mathematical Models
3. Numerical Methods

Figure 59: Investment Regression Analysis process Inputs, Outputs, and Tools & Techniques.

Figure 60: Investment Valuation Analysis process Inputs, Outputs, and Tools & Techniques.

Investment Variation Analysis
1. Portfolio Snapshot
2. Benefit Risk Document
3. Cost Risk Document
1. Investment Regression Document
1. Investment Variation Document
1. Statistical Techniques
2. Mathematical Models
3. Numerical Methods

Investment Model Definition
1. Asset Category Data
2. Data Quality Document
3. Data Consistency Document
4. Data Stability Document
5. Benefit Risk Document
6. Cost Risk Document
7. Action Impact Document
8. Inaction Impact Document
9. Technical Capability Document
10. Feasibility Document
11. Current Maturity Document
12. Future Maturity Document
13. Investment Regression Document
14. Investment Variation Document
15. Valuation Model
16. Investment Quality Document
17. Investment Reliability Document
1. Investment Model
1. Risk Analysis
2. Mathematical Models
3. Numerical Methods
4. Statistical Techniques
5. Requirements Analysis

Figure 61: Investment Variation Analysis process Inputs, Outputs, and Tools & Techniques.

Figure 62: Investment Model Definition process Inputs, Outputs, and Tools & Techniques.

Investment Regression Analysis

Investment Regression Analysis is a common technique used to analyze multi-dimensional data sets. Regression Analysis can readily incorporate both values and uncertainties. Investment Regression Analysis can be used to determine optimal weights to put against category values. This can be used to create a simple linear model for the Investment Value.

Alternatively, Investment Regression Analysis can be part of the Model itself. In this manner, the Investment Value may be determined by performing an Investment Regression Analysis against some of the data fields. In this respect, the Investment Regression Analysis is incorporated into the model itself.

Investment Valuation Analysis

Investment Valuation Analysis is used to compute the inherent value of the investment. This analysis examines the intrinsic value as well as the expected future change in value.

The results of Investment Regression Analysis may be used to estimate the expected future value of the asset. In addition, we may compute the present value of the future returns in order to compute the present value of the investment.

Investment Variation Analysis

Investment Variation Analysis is used to compute the uncertainty of the Investment Value. This section has presented several measures of uncertainty in the fields. These may be combined together to compute the overall uncertainty for the Investment Value.

Uncertainties may be combined and propagated using the standard error propagation analysis. For example, let $x \pm \Delta x$ and $y \pm \Delta y$ be two fields. Let $f(x, y)$ be the Investment Model. The error in the Investment Value is

$$\Delta f^2 = \left(\frac{\partial f}{\partial x}\right)^2 \Delta x^2 + \left(\frac{\partial f}{\partial y}\right)^2 \Delta y^2 \qquad \text{6-1}$$

Investment Model Definition

Investment Model Definition is the specific mathematical model or function used to compute the Investment Value for each asset. This model incorporates all of the information discussed in this section. For each investment, the model will compute one or more Investment Values and their associated uncertainties or errors.

There are many potential models that may be used to compute Investment Value. The particular model used for a given portfolio should be custom tailored to reflect the factors important to the portfolio. Furthermore, we should always be mindful that values computed from different models are not comparable.

7 System Model

The System Model is a model used to quantify the value, uncertainty, and performance of systems of investments grouped together. Systems are groups of investments that should be analyzed together because the value of the group may differ from the sum of the constituent parts.

In many cases, the value of the system is thought to be greater than the sum of the constituent investments. This additional value represents a value achieved from investments cooperating together to produce more efficient results than the individual investments would achieve in isolation.

Alternatively, some systems may have a lower value that the sum of the constituent investments. This may be due to situations such as inefficiencies, overlapping functions, and inconsistencies between investments.

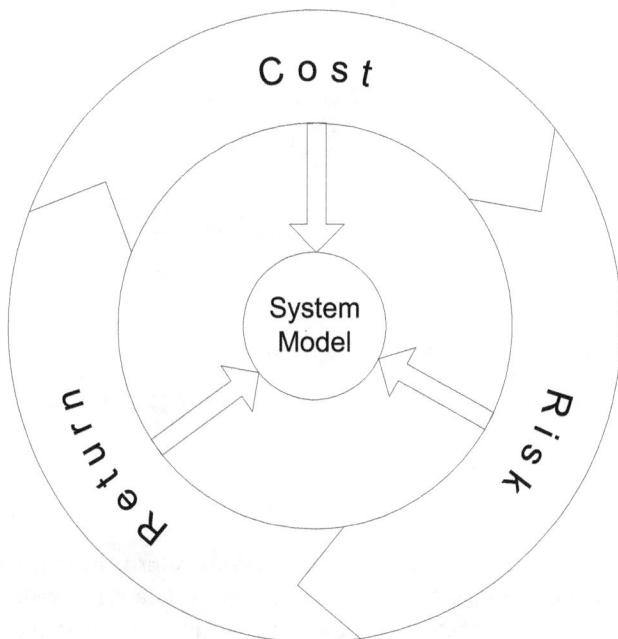

Figure 63: The Portfolio Model is based on factors such as Compliance, Risk, Cost, and Return.

The System Model is the result of System Cost Analysis, System Risk Analysis, System Return Analysis, and System Model Analysis. This is in many ways similar to the structure around the Portfolio Model. This is due to the fact that both Systems and Portfolios are fundamentally groups of investments. However, Portfolios may contain entire Systems as components.

System Cost Analysis reviews the present and future costs for a system of investments. These processes incorporate the time value of money as a principal ingredient of their analysis.

System Risk Analysis examines uncertainties in the values computed from the System Model. These processes examine system risk as well as system sensitivity.

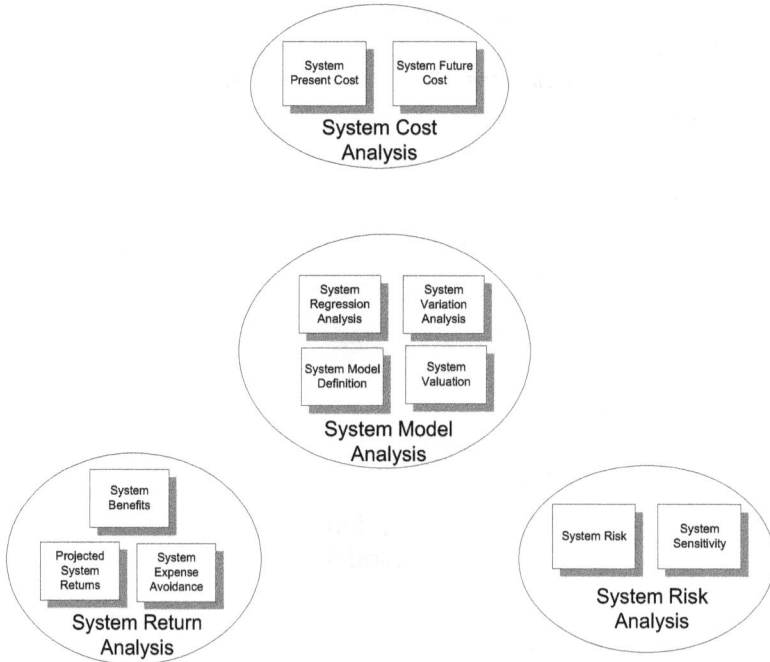

Figure 64: The Portfolio Model process.

System Return Analysis quantifies the system return. In particular, the system benefits are quantified. The system benefits are the additional (or reduced) value associated with the system of investments above the sum of the constituent investments.

System Cost Analysis

System Cost Analysis in the System Model analyzes the present and anticipated future costs of the investments. The costs are used to quantify the return during System Return Analysis.

System Present Cost
1. Investment Model
2. System Evaluations
1. System Present Cost
1. Performance Models
2. Risk Models
3. Taxation Issues

System Future Cost
1. Investment Model
2. System Evaluations
1. System Future Cost
1. Performance Models
2. Risk Models
3. Taxation Issues

Figure 65: System Present Cost process Inputs, Outputs, and Tools & Techniques.

Figure 66: System Future Cost process Inputs, Outputs, and Tools & Techniques.

System Present Cost

System Present Cost examines the current and prior cost of the investments in the system. This analysis includes both fixed and variable costs to evaluate the present cost of the investment. The present cost is useful to the System Model for later computations of ROI.

System Present Cost uses Performance and Risk Models to assist with the identification and quantification of current and past costs. In addition, this process examines potential Taxation Issues to effectively determine the cost.

System Future Cost

System Future Cost addresses the present value of anticipated future costs of an investment. Future costs are typically discounted when computing their present value because of the time vale of money. System Future Cost examines known costs, potential costs, and estimates unknown costs.

Similar to System Present Cost, this processes used Performance and Risk Models and examines Taxation Issues. These issues are all evaluated in the light of the time value of money to determine the present value of the system.

System Risk Analysis

System Risk Analysis quantifies the uncertainties in the system values. The values are the values associated with the composite system of investments, taken as a whole. The risk is the uncertainty in this composite value.

System Risk

The System Risk process quantifies the uncertainties in the System Values. These uncertainties are computed using similar error propagation models as in the Investment Model. The value for a system is often expressed as

$$S = \Delta + \sum_k I_k$$

where I_k is the value of the kth investment in the system and Δ is the additional value associated with the system as a whole. Δ is computed during the System Benefits process.

System Sensitivity

System Sensitivity Analysis examines how sensitive the system values are with respect to perturbations in the underlying investment values. Sensitivity analysis attempts to discern how sensitive the future value of the system is due to the uncertainties in the underlying investment values.

Linear system valuation models similar to the one above typically do not exhibit a great deal of sensitivity. However, nonlinear models can provide a great deal of sensitivity, especially in the vicinity of singular points.

System Risk
1. Investment Model
2. System Evaluations
1. System Risk
1. Performance Models
2. Risk Models

Figure 67: System Risk process Inputs, Outputs, and Tools & Techniques.

System Sensitivity
1. Investment Model
2. System Evaluations
1. System Sensitivity
1. Performance Models
2. Risk Models

Figure 68: System Sensitivity process Inputs, Outputs, and Tools & Techniques.

System Return Analysis

System Return Analysis examines the potential returns that the system may incur. The returns may be in the form of System Benefits, System Expense Avoidance, or Projected System Returns. The processes in this group examine and attempt to quantify system returns.

System Benefits

System Benefits reviews the benefits that each investment brings to the overall system. The benefit is often quantified a value over and above the sum of the values of the constituent systems.

System Expense Avoidance

System Expense Avoidance quantifies the savings the investments bring to the system. For example, a system of investments targeted toward regulatory compliance avoids the expense of costly fines that would have been levied but for the investments. This expense avoidance is a system benefit and is quantified in this process.

System Benefits
1. Investment Model
2. System Evaluations
1. System Benefits
1. Requirements Analysis

System Expense Avoidance
1. Investment Model
2. System Evaluations
3. System Future Cost
1. System Expense Avoidance

Projected System Returns
1. Investment Model
2. System Future Costs
1. Projected System Returns
1. Performance Models
2. Risk Models

Figure 69: System Benefits process Inputs, Outputs, and Tools & Techniques.

Figure 70: System Expense Avoidance process Inputs, Outputs, and Tools & Techniques.

Figure 71: Projected System Returns process Inputs, Outputs, and Tools & Techniques.

Projected System Returns

Projected System Returns estimates the expected future returns for the system of investments. Estimating future returns is important as these may be measured against actual returns. This process allows for continual improvement of the estimating models.

This is important as portfolio rationalization may recommend new systems or investment be created in order to increase portfolio efficiency. The better the predictive models, the more reliable the results, and the more efficient the portfolio rationalization process becomes.

System Model Analysis

The System Model Analysis combines the System Cost Analysis, System Risk Analysis, and System Return Analysis to formulate the System Model. The System Model is a mathematical representation of the value of the system. The model specifies, mathematically, how to compute the value of the system based on the values of the constituent investments and the system benefits.

System Regression Analysis

System Regression analysis is a statistical technique for creating models from data in a scatter-plot format. We may perform a least-squares best-fit of the scatter-plot data, and then use this fit to attempt to predict the future values of the system. Alternatively, we may interpolate how the value of the system benefits may change as the values of the underlying investments vary.

System Variation Analysis

System Variation Analysis examines the sensitivity and uncertainty in the regression analysis. These factors contribute to the overall uncertainty in the values produced from the System Model.

System Variation Analysis uses Performance and Risk models to estimate the uncertainty from the System Regression Analysis. This process reviews a wide range of system related information to conduct the uncertainty analysis.

System Valuation

System Valuation identifies potential mathematical expressions for quantifying system value. In particular, this process examines the regression analysis from the System Regression Analysis along with the System Variation Analysis. Taken in conjunction, these represent potential system valuation models along with the error analysis for the model.

System Model Definition

System Model Definition reviews the mathematical models from System Valuation to determine the overall models used to compute the system values. This culminates in mathematical models used to compute the values of the system.

System Model Definition reviews many system related information including System Risk, System Sensitivity, Present System Cost, Future System Cost, System benefits, System Expense Avoidance, Projected System Returns, System Regression Analysis, System Variation, and System Valuation. All of this information can contribute to formulating a System Model appropriate for the system of investments under consideration.

Furthermore, we can have a System Model for every system of investments in the portfolio. The System Phase may be repeated for each system in the portfolio producing a unique System Model for each. When we discuss the System Model in the Portfolio Phase, we are referring to the collection of all System Models.

System Regression Analysis

1. System Risk
2. System Sensitivity
3. System Present Cost
4. System Future Cost
5. System Benefits
6. System Expense Avoidance
7. Projected System Returns

1. System Regression Analysis

1. Performance Models
2. Risk Models

Figure 72: System Regression Analysis process Inputs, Outputs, and Tools & Techniques.

System Variation Analysis

1. System Risk
2. System Sensitivity
3. System Present Cost
4. System Future Cost
5. System Benefits
6. System Expense Avoidance
7. Projected System Returns
8. System Regression Analysis
9. Investment Valuation

1. System Variation

1. Performance Models
2. Risk Models

Figure 73: System Variation Analysis process Inputs, Outputs, and Tools & Techniques.

System Valuation Analysis

1. System Risk
2. System Sensitivity
3. Present System Cost
4. Future System Cost
5. System Benefits
6. System Expense Avoidance
7. Projected System Returns
8. System Regression Analysis

1. System Valuation

1. Performance Models
2. Risk Models

Figure 74: System Valuation Analysis process Inputs, Outputs, and Tools & Techniques.

System Model Definition

1. System Risk
2. System Sensitivity
3. Present System Cost
4. Future System Cost
5. System Benefits
6. System Expense Avoidance
7. Projected System Returns
8. System Regression Analysis
9. System Variation
10. System Valuation

1. System Model

1. Performance Models
2. Risk Models

Figure 75: System Model Definition process Inputs, Outputs, and Tools & Techniques.

8 Portfolio Model

The Portfolio Model is a model used to quantify the value, uncertainty, and performance of the portfolio as a whole. Just as with Business Value, there may be several values assigned to the portfolio, each of which measures a different aspect of the portfolio. By evaluating different aspects of the portfolio separately, we can better understand the multi-dimensional nature typical of non-financial portfolios.

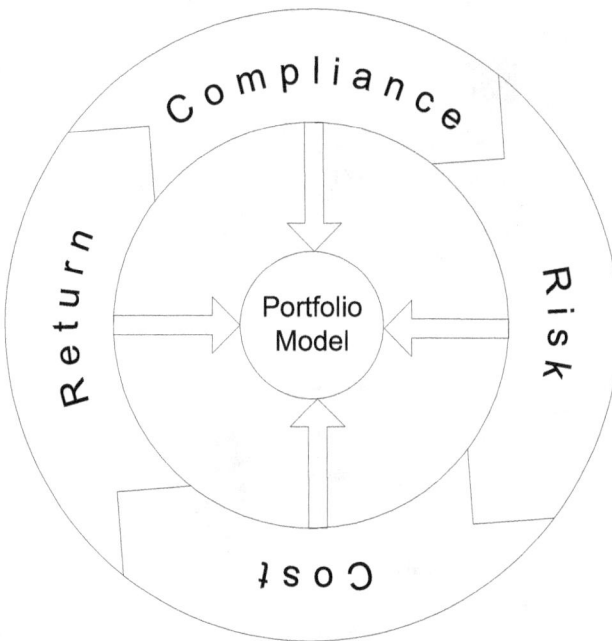

Figure 76: The Portfolio Model is based on factors such as Compliance, Risk, Cost, and Return.

The Portfolio Model examines four main areas: Compliance, Risk, Cost, and Return. These are the main ingredients to understanding the value, uncertainty, and performance of the portfolio as a whole. Each of these areas is further segmented into individual sub-areas. These sub-areas are not intended to represent an exhaustive list of related knowledge; rather, they are intended to specify common elements used to evaluate their corresponding area.

Compliance Analysis addresses how well the portfolio conforms to expectations. Compliance is measured in terms of the overall Portfolio Performance, regulatory issues, and portfolio governance. Compliance measures help to identify where the portfolio diverges from expectations.

Portfolio Risk Analysis examines the uncertainties associated with the values from the Portfolio Model. This group examines the overall portfolio risk as well as the sensitivity of the risk. Portfolio Sensitivity analysis is important in determining the potential impact of uncertainties in the portfolio values.

Portfolio Cost Analysis examines the present and future costs associated with the portfolio. These processes account for the time value of money to better understand the present value of future portfolio returns.

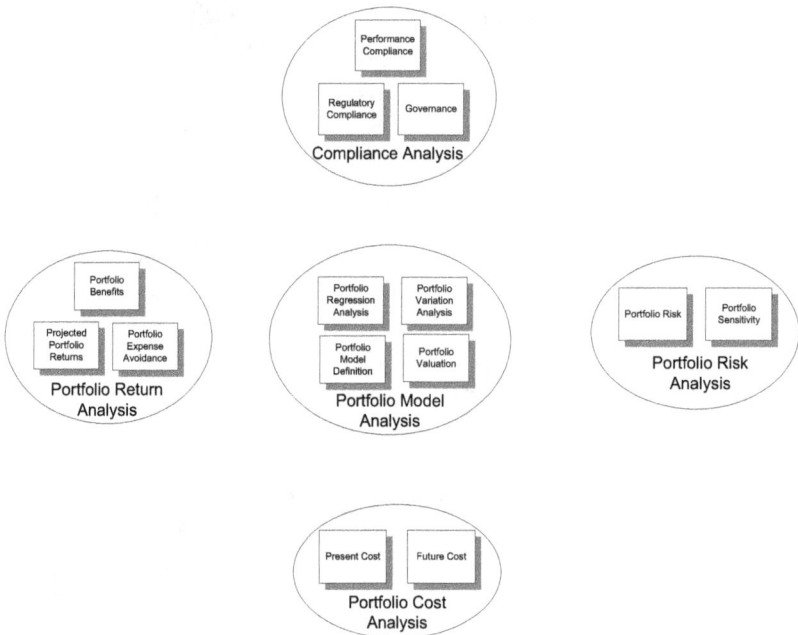

Figure 77: The Portfolio Model process.

Portfolio Return Analysis quantifies the portfolio return. Return may be measured in two ways. First, return may be measured as direct benefit to the portfolio. Second, return may be measured as avoidance of expense. Understanding these cost savings realized through reduction of expenses is an important aspect of portfolio rationalization.

Compliance Analysis

Compliance Analysis examines how well the portfolio is conforming to expectations. There are many different potential measures of compliance. Three common compliance measures we discuss are the overall Performance Compliance, Regulatory Compliance, and Governance. These three measures of the compliance of a portfolio to expectations provide a basis for an overall evaluation of the compliance health of the portfolio.

Performance Compliance
1. Performance Expectations
1. Performance Compliance
1. Alignment Models 2. Performance Models 3. Risk Models

Governance
1. Business Strategy 2. Business Vision 3. System Evaluations
1. Governance Document
1. Alignment Models 2. Performance Models 3. Risk Models

Regulatory Compliance
1. Statutes & Regulations
1. Regulatory Compliance
1. Requirements Analysis 2. Legal Research

Figure 78: Performance Compliance process Inputs, Outputs, and Tools & Techniques.

Figure 79: Governance process Inputs, Outputs, and Tools & Techniques.

Figure 80: Regulatory Compliance process Inputs, Outputs, and Tools & Techniques.

Performance Compliance

Performance Compliance measures how the portfolio has performed with respect to an expected or projected value. Past examinations of the portfolio produced expected costs from the Future Cost process. Current examinations measure the actual costs incurred. These past predictions can be measured against actual performance to determine how well the actual performance has aligned with the projections.

Regulatory Compliance

Regulatory Compliance is a fundamental issue in portfolio rationalization. Unlike financial portfolios, regulatory issues often drive strategy and portfolio management decisions. Compliance with Federal, State, and Local regulations is a critical issue for many organizations. This process examines the compliance of the portfolio with these regulations to determine if course corrections are warranted. In addition, this process reviews regulations to determine if they still apply to the portfolio investments.

Governance

Portfolio Governance addresses the compliance of the portfolio management with the governance strategy of the organization. Compliance with the governance strategy is essential in order to assure that the portfolio remains aligned with the strategy of the organization. The Portfolio Rationalization Process cannot reliably produce good recommendations if the Portfolio Rationalization Process itself is not compliant with the organizational strategy.

Portfolio Risk
1. Investment Model
2. System Model
3. System Evaluations
4. Business Strategy
5. Business Vision
1. Portfolio Risk
1. Alignment Models
2. Performance Models
3. Risk Models

Figure 81: Portfolio Risk process Inputs, Outputs, and Tools & Techniques.

Portfolio Sensitivity
1. Investment Model
2. System Model
3. System Evaluations
4. Business Strategy
5. Business Vision
1. Portfolio Sensitivity
1. Alignment Models
2. Performance Models
3. Risk Models

Figure 82: Portfolio Sensitivity process Inputs, Outputs, and Tools & Techniques.

Portfolio Risk Analysis

Portfolio Risk Analysis examines and quantifies the uncertainties in the portfolio values. These uncertainties are similar to the uncertainties in the Business Value from the Investment Model. Just as in that case, the Portfolio Values themselves are useless without an understanding of the associated uncertainties.

Portfolio Risk

The Portfolio Risk process quantifies the uncertainties in the Portfolio Values. These uncertainties are computed using similar error propagation models as in the Investment Model. The uncertainties are used to specify the Portfolio Value with an associated error such as $1.52M±0.02M. The nature of the uncertainties is that the true value lies on some probability distribution characterized by the value and uncertainty. For example, if the value is $1.52M±0.02M, this indicates that the true value lies on a Gaussian distribution, centered on the value $1.52M, and with standard deviation 0.02M.

Analysis of stochastic variables may be effective to Portfolio Risk. A stochastic process is a process that incorporates a random element. The model of a stochastic process will contain one or more stochastic variables. Monte Carlo simulations can be used effectively to analyze potential outcomes of the model based on evolving the present values of the variables. In financial portfolio analysis, these techniques lead to models such as the Black and Scholes option pricing model.

Portfolio Sensitivity

Portfolio Sensitivity analysis examines how sensitive the values and predictions are with respect to perturbations in their values. For instance, a Portfolio Model may make several performance predictions based on the Portfolio Values and their uncertainties. However, a model combining several of these uncertain values together may be sensitive to small perturbations.

Portfolio Sensitivity analysis is important in portfolio rationalization as it identifies when the portfolio is sensitive to uncertainties in the Investment Values. Predictions based on models that are highly sensitive to the Investment Values may lead to unpredictable results. When a model is identified as sensitive, additional care should be taken to assure that predictions from the model are reliable.

Portfolio Cost Analysis

Portfolio Cost Analysis in the Portfolio Model examines the present and anticipated costs of the investments. These costs are an important factor when evaluating the benefits of the investment to the portfolio. The results of Cost Analysis are factored into the Portfolio Model in order to properly understand the value of each investment to the portfolio.

Portfolio Present Cost

Portfolio Present Cost reviews the current and past cost of the investments. This analysis includes both fixed and variable costs to evaluate the present cost of the investment. The present cost is useful to the Portfolio Model for later computations of ROI. Present Costs are usually readily computed as many of these are investment costs that have been realized.

Portfolio Future Cost

Portfolio Future Cost addresses the present value of future costs of an investment. Due to the time value of money, future costs are typically discounted when computing their present value. Future Cost examines known costs, potential costs, and estimates unknown costs. Future Cost also examines disposition effects as well as taxation issues.

Portfolio Future Costs are not as easy to compute as Portfolio Present Costs. Future Costs have not been realized and there may be some degree of speculation as to whether the cost will be incurred at all. In addition, Future Cost addresses unknown issues such as the cost an investment may incur due to an increase in oil prices. Because it is impossible to know if oil prices will increase and if so, to what degree, Future Cost analysis does not present precise values. Instead, Future Cost examines potential scenarios and their impact.

Portfolio Present Cost
1. Investment Model
2. System Model
3. System Evaluations
4. Business Strategy
5. Business Vision
1. Portfolio Present Cost
1. Alignment Models
2. Performance Models
3. Risk Models
4. Taxation Issues

Figure 83: Portfolio Present Cost process Inputs, Outputs, and Tools & Techniques.

Portfolio Future Cost
1. Investment Model
2. System Model
3. System Evaluations
4. Business Strategy
5. Business Vision
1. Portfolio Future Cost
1. Alignment Models
2. Performance Models
3. Risk Models
4. Taxation Issues

Figure 84: Portfolio Future Cost process Inputs, Outputs, and Tools & Techniques.

Portfolio Return Analysis

Portfolio Return Analysis examines the potential returns that the portfolio may receive from the investments. The returns may be in the form of Portfolio Benefits, Portfolio Expense Avoidance, or Projected Portfolio Returns. Returns do not need to be financially quantifiable. For example, Portfolio Benefits may include the benefits of regulatory compliance or improved worker retention.

Portfolio Benefits
1. Investment Model
2. System Model
3. System Evaluations
4. Business Strategy
5. Business Vision
1. Portfolio Benefits
1. Requirements Analysis

Figure 85: Portfolio Benefits process Inputs, Outputs, and Tools & Techniques.

Portfolio Expense Aviodance
1. Investment Model
2. System Model
3. System Evaluations
4. Portfolio Future Cost
1. Portfolio Expense Avoidance
1. Alignment Models

Figure 86: Portfolio Expense Avoidance process Inputs, Outputs, and Tools & Techniques.

Projected Portfolio Returns
1. Investment Model
2. System Model
3. System Evaluations
4. Portfolio Future Cost
1. Projected Portfolio Returns
1. Alignment Models
2. Performance Models
3. Risk Models

Figure 87: Projected Portfolio Returns process Inputs, Outputs, and Tools & Techniques.

Portfolio Benefits

Portfolio Benefits reviews the benefits that each investment brings to the overall portfolio. This does not necessarily need to align with the purpose or product of the investment itself.

For example, a tree planting program in a portfolio of green initiatives benefits the portfolio because this program is aligned with the strategic purpose of the portfolio. However, the same program in a portfolio for employee satisfaction may benefit the portfolio by increasing morale. In the first case, the primary product of the program, newly planted trees, is aligned with the purpose of the portfolio. In the second case, the newly planted trees are not aligned with the primary, but the investment still adds value to the overall portfolio.

Portfolio Expense Avoidance

Portfolio Expense Avoidance is another way that an investment may benefit the overall portfolio. Here, an investment may incur a cost while preventing another cost. For example, a regulatory compliance project may cost $1M annually, but this compliance may prevent $5M in fines. The investment does not generate positive value by itself, but may add value to the portfolio by avoiding other costs. These potential cost savings may be viewed as a return on the investment.

Projected Portfolio Returns

Some investments do not have benefits that are easy to determine. For example, marketing campaigns are important for branding the corporate image, but it can be difficult to determine exactly how much value a given campaign actually produces.

Projected portfolio Returns allow for flexibility in estimating the potential value of an investment. This process may be used in cases when the value is hard to measure or in cases where the value is simply unknown at present.

For instance, the sales of a newly developed product are not known at present, but will be known in the future. Projected Portfolio Returns may be used to estimate the return from this investment and inserted into the Portfolio Model.

Portfolio Model Analysis

The Portfolio Model Analysis is the meeting of these analyses to form a model of the overall portfolio. The model begins with an understanding of the cost, return, uncertainty, and compliance. From these ingredients, the Rationalization Manager formulates the Portfolio Model.

This model is intended to quantify the value(s) of the overall portfolio. The model may be as simple as the sum of the values of each of the constituent investments. However, typically the Portfolio Model is not this simple and the value of the whole is different than the sum of its parts.

The Portfolio Model can use a wide variety of techniques. Specific situations require tailoring the process to meet the individual requirements of the organization. However, many cases commonly use these processes to complete the task. Portfolio Regression Analysis is often used to create basic Mathematical Models that can be used to extrapolate Investment Values over time, cost, return, or other variables. These models are then used to perform a Portfolio Valuation Analysis that identifies the potential value(s) that may be used to measure the Portfolio Performance. Finally, Portfolio Model Definition uses these value(s) to specify a particular computational model for the portfolio.

Portfolio Regression Analysis

Portfolio Regression Analysis is a statistical technique for creating models from data in a scatter-plot. As an example, the daily closing price of a stock may be plotted over some period of time. The data is a scatter plot of individual data points. From this we may find the least-squares best-fit of the data to a straight line, and then use this line to attempt to predict the future values of the stock. The process of taking the original data and producing the best-fit straight line is a form of regression analysis.

Portfolio Regression Analysis may be used to model the values of the investments. This may be similar to the example above where we wish to estimate the value of the investment over time. However, we can also use regression analysis to extrapolate values over other variables such as cost, return, or even compliance. In each case we create a scatter plot of the investment data and then compute a best-fit curve. What values we choose and what type of curve we fit to (line, parabola, sinusoid) are up to the skill, art, and experience of the Rationalization Manager.

The raw data for Portfolio Regression Analysis comes from the results of Compliance Analysis, Portfolio Risk Analysis, Cost Analysis, and Return Analysis. These analyses are not simply performed in isolation. Rather, each of these is conducted with the purpose of gathering fundamental data as an input to the Portfolio Regression Analysis process.

Portfolio Variation Analysis

Portfolio Variation Analysis examines sensitivity concerns of the models produced from the Portfolio Regression Analysis. Some of these sensitivity concerns were examined in the Portfolio Sensitivity process. Here, the Sensitivity in the particular Portfolio Models identified from regression analysis is examined.

This is important because the value of the predictions from the regression models is dependent on how sensitive these models are to perturbations. The regression models are formulated based on the Investment Values. However, these values are subject to uncertainties. These uncertainties may lead to unreliable models if the models are highly sensitive to perturbations in the values of the investments.

In particular, Monte Carlo techniques may be used to generate investment data sets where the Investment Values are determined from a probability distribution based on the investment value and uncertainty. Regression analysis may be performed on each of these generated data sets, yielding different regression models. The various models may be analyzed together to determine how sensitive the models are to perturbations in the underlying investment data values.

Portfolio Valuation Analysis

Portfolio Valuation Analysis examines the Mathematical Models from the Portfolio Regression Analysis to identify potential values that may make good measures of portfolio value. For example, Portfolio Regression Analysis may identify a model for the 'number of users' for a wide range of investments. Based on this, Portfolio Valuation Analysis may identify 'total number of users' as a potential portfolio value.

Portfolio Valuation Analysis should identify several potential values for the portfolio. The values do not need to have any relation to one another. We may have a value for 'total number of users' and another value for 'total workdays without injury' for the same portfolio. However, we may also combine values to generate new values such as 'total workdays without injury / total number of users'. Again, it is up to the Rationalization Manager to use good judgment in identifying potential portfolio values.

Portfolio Model Definition

Based on the results of the Portfolio Valuation Analysis, the Portfolio Model Definition identifies a set of values intended to measure the performance of the portfolio. The Rationalization Manager may simply select values straight from the Portfolio Valuation Analysis, or may use these as inputs for a more complicated model. The model may incorporate some form of Computational Intelligence to adapt to changing situations, automatically incorporate new variables, or even modify the underlying model.

Portfolio Regression Analysis
1. Performance Compliance
2. Governance Document
3. Regulatory Compliance
4. Portfolio Risk
5. Portfolio Sensitivity
6. Present Portfolio Cost
7. Future Portfolio Cost
8. Portfolio Benefits
9. Portfolio Expense Avoidance
10. Projected Portfolio Returns

1. Portfolio Regression Analysis
1. Alignment Models
2. Performance Models
3. Risk Models

Figure 88: Portfolio Regression Analysis process Inputs, Outputs, and Tools & Techniques.

Portfolio Variation Analysis
1. Performance Compliance
2. Governance Document
3. Regulatory Compliance
4. Portfolio Risk
5. Portfolio Sensitivity
6. Portfolio Present Cost
7. Portfolio Future Cost
8. Portfolio Benefits
9. Portfolio Expense Avoidance
10. Projected Portfolio Returns
11. Portfolio Regression Analysis
12. System Valuation

1. Portfolio Variation
1. Alignment Models
2. Performance Models
3. Risk Models

Figure 89: Portfolio Variation Analysis process Inputs, Outputs, and Tools & Techniques.

Portfolio Valuation Analysis
1. Performance Compliance
2. Governance Document
3. Regulatory Compliance
4. Portfolio Risk
5. Portfolio Sensitivity
6. Present Portfolio Cost
7. Future Portfolio Cost
8. Portfolio Benefits
9. Portfolio Expense Avoidance
10. Projected Portfolio Returns
11. Portfolio Regression Analysis

1. Portfolio Valuation
1. Alignment Models
2. Performance Models
3. Risk Models

Figure 90: Portfolio Valuation Analysis process Inputs, Outputs, and Tools & Techniques.

Portfolio Model Definition
1. Performance Compliance
2. Governance Document
3. Regulatory Compliance
4. Portfolio Risk
5. Portfolio Sensitivity
6. Present Portfolio Cost
7. Future Portfolio Cost
8. Portfolio Benefits
9. Portfolio Expense Avoidance
10. Projected Portfolio Returns
11. Portfolio Regression Analysis
12. Portfolio Variation
13. Portfolio Valuation

1. Portfolio Model
1. Alignment Models
2. Performance Models
3. Risk Models

Figure 91: Portfolio Model Definition process Inputs, Outputs, and Tools & Techniques.

9 Rationalization Model

The Rationalization Model is a model is used to identify investments that are appropriate targets for rationalization. This model may be a mathematical model, or it may be a manual process. In either case, the Rationalization Model reviews the performance of the investments and portfolio in conjunction with the System Requirements to determine which investments are best suited for rationalization.

The Rationalization Model is broken down by system, requirements, and resource categories into three pairs: redundant v. gap, obsolete v. reuse, and merger v. division. Each of these pairs is opposite in effect and each presents an opportunity to migrate the portfolio in different directions.

Redundancy/Gap compiles the requirements, purpose, and/or functionality of the portfolio investments to determine if there is overlap between the investments or if there are functionality gaps that should be filled. Redundancy looks for overlaps while Gap looks for holes.

Obsolete/Reuse examines the requirements, purpose, and/or functionality of the portfolio investments to see if any of the investments are obsolete or may be reused. This may be true for an entire investment or for some constituent component. Because individual components of an investment are examined, it is possible that an investment may have both opportunities for reuse and be obsolete. For example, a legacy payroll system may be overall obsolete, but there may be individual software components that may be reused in new systems.

Merger/Division checks the investments to determine if there are opportunities to achieve economies of scale. Merger looks at the portfolio investments and determines if cost savings may be realized by combining two or more investments together. Division has the opposite effect and examines if cost savings may be realized by dividing investments into multiple smaller units.

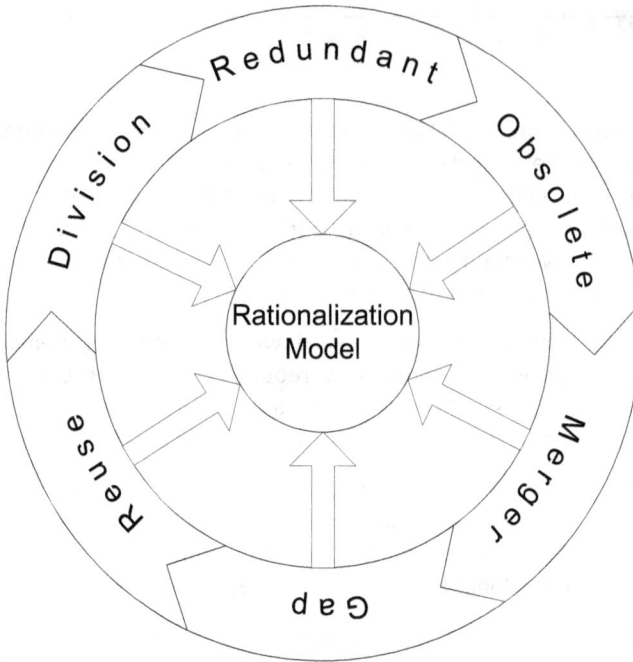

Figure 92: The Rationalization Model is based on redundancy v. gap, obsolescence v. reuse, and merger v. divide.

Redundancy/Gap

Each of the investments in a portfolio has some set of underlying requirements, purpose, or functionality. This analysis examines the combined effect of all of these across the entire portfolio. Based on this, we can see if there is some overlap in the investments or some gap that should be filled.

An investment does not need to be completely redundant to benefit from rationalization. We may find that two investments have different purposes but have some degree of overlap. It is this overlap that we may wish to rationalize by eliminating the redundant component from one of the investments. Alternatively, we might remove the overlap from both investments and create a new investment that focuses only on the overlapping area. Moreover, we may find that the redundancy is desired and leave the investments as is.

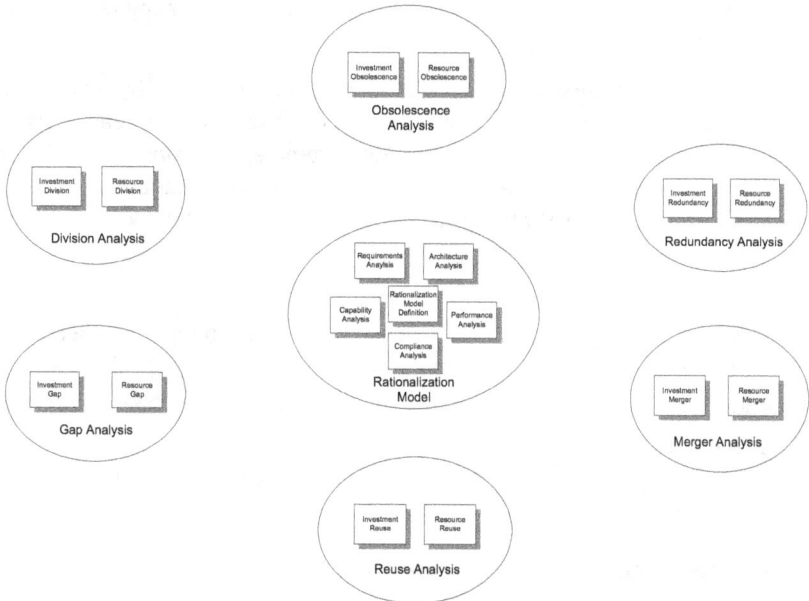

Figure 93: The Rationalization Model processes.

Obsolete/Reuse

These processes examine the investments in the portfolio to determine if there are any obsolete components or any opportunities for reuse. Reuse is especially important in software systems as these are often designed with reuse in mind. Cost savings may be achieved by constructing a single component and sharing this system across several investments.

We also need to check the portfolio for obsolete investments. Investments may become obsolete for a wide variety of reasons. Investments may be obsolete because they are no longer needed (old products that have been retired), they no longer serve their intended purpose (regulatory project where the underlying regulation is repealed), or simply no longer fit with the strategic direction of the organization.

It may be that the entire investment is not either obsolete or reused. This analysis examines the components making up the investment to determine if there is opportunity. Because of this, an investment may be marked as obsolete because there are some obsolete components, while at the same time marked as reusable because some components may be reused elsewhere.

Merger/Division

The Merger and Division processes examine the portfolio investments and identify opportunities to realize savings through economies of scale. These processes are especially important during a company merger where different portfolios are combined together.

Investment Mergers may achieve economies of scale by combining multiple investments into a single unit. This can reduce overhead costs by eliminating underused elements. For example, merging two similar projects may eliminate the need for one of the project managers, or some of the project staff. Alternatively, merging the projects may require less equipment resources.

Division is useful when there are diseconomies of scale. In some situations there may be a savings achieved by dividing a larger unit into smaller units. For example, the number of communication lines in a project with n people is $\frac{n(n+1)}{2}$. By dividing this into two projects, each of the new projects has fewer communication lines. This may increase the overall efficiency of the effort, especially when the project is made up of distinct, independent components.

Requirements, Purpose, and Functionality
Each of the three pairs of processes above examines investment requirements, purpose, and/or functionality. Each of these six processes examines these aspects in terms of both the investments and resources. Investments and resources are further broken down and described below.

Investment

Project/Program

Investments may be examined in terms of individual projects or programs. Here, the project/program requirements, purpose, and functionality should be examined. This is done for the entire project/program, but the individual sub-units of the project/program are also examined.

Product/Process/Service

Investments may be examined for the products, processes, or services the investment produces. These may be the result of a project or program, or they may be part of an ongoing operation. In either case, these results are examined by each of the six processes mentioned above to identify potential rationalization targets.

Vendor

Vendors may also be examined by these processes. There may be opportunities to consolidate or eliminate vendors and achieve cost savings through preferred customer discounts. Alternatively, we may find that adding new vendors is appropriate in order to relieve supply chain problems. In any case, vendor relationships should be reviewed by each of these processes.

Contract

The investments may have contractual obligations tied to them. This is another potential source for rationalization targets. Here, contractual obligations may be reviewed under the above processes to identify potential savings. Contractual obligations are typically not as easy to modify as they usually require permission of the contracting parties. However, they should still be examined as potential rationalization targets.

Resources

Personnel

Investments are often supported by company personnel. The rationalization process should examine the personnel requirements to determine if there are opportunities to reduce the workforce. For example, in a software portfolio, we may find several database developers on each project in the portfolio. We may be able to achieve savings by consolidating all database developers into a single data development unit and requiring each software project to matrix with this unit for data developers.

Equipment

Equipment is another source of rationalization targets. Investments often have equipment resources required for their operation. It may be the case that there is extra equipment available from one investment that can be used in another. We may achieve savings by better distributing this equipment across the investments.

Infrastructure

Investments may have substantial infrastructure that may be a target for rationalization. Computer networks, routers, databases, roads, water supply, power, and telecommunications are just a few examples of infrastructures that may support an investment. Any of these may be reviewed by these six processes to identify potential rationalization targets.

Licenses

Licenses are also a source of rationalization targets. This is particularly true in the IT arenas where software licenses are abundant and may be transferrable between different units within the same organization. However, not all software licenses are reusable in this way and care should be taken to consult the actual license agreement to determine if these are proper rationalization targets.

Facilities

Facilities may be rationalization targets as well. Manufacturing portfolios may have several facilities and some may be underutilized. In these cases the above processes can examine the facility resources and identify potential rationalization targets.

Investment Obsolescence
1. Portfolio Valuation
2. Portfolio Performance
3. Business Strategy
4. Business Vision
5. System Evaluations
6. Strategic Alignments
7. Strategic Recommendations
1. Investment Obsolescence Rules
2. Investment Requirements
1. Fitness Models
2. Risk Analysis
3. Computational Intelligence
4. Numerical Methods
5. Mathematical Models
6. Requirements Matrices

Figure 94: Investment Obsolescence process Inputs, Outputs, and Tools & Techniques.

Resource Obsolescence
1. Portfolio Valuation
2. Portfolio Performance
3. Business Strategy
4. Business Vision
5. System Evaluations
6. Strategic Alignments
7. Strategic Recommendations
1. Resource Obsolescence Rules
2. Resource Requirements
1. Fitness Models
2. Risk Analysis
3. Computational Intelligence
4. Numerical Methods
5. Mathematical Models
6. Requirements Matrices

Figure 95: Resource Obsolescence process Inputs, Outputs, and Tools & Techniques.

Investment Reuse
1. Portfolio Valuation
2. Portfolio Performance
3. Business Strategy
4. Business Vision
5. System Evaluations
6. Strategic Alignments
7. Strategic Recommendations
1. Investment Reuse Rules
2. Investment Requirements
1. Fitness Models
2. Risk Analysis
3. Computational Intelligence
4. Numerical Methods
5. Mathematical Models
6. Requirements Matrices

Figure 96: Investment Reuse process Inputs, Outputs, and Tools & Techniques.

Resource Reuse
1. Portfolio Valuation
2. Portfolio Performance
3. Business Strategy
4. Business Vision
5. System Evaluations
6. Strategic Alignments
7. Strategic Recommendations
1. Resource Reuse Rules
2. Resource Requirements
1. Fitness Models
2. Risk Analysis
3. Computational Intelligence
4. Numerical Methods
5. Mathematical Models
6. Requirements Matrices

Figure 97: Resource Reuse process Inputs, Outputs, and Tools & Techniques.

Investment Redundancy
1. Portfolio Valuation
2. Portfolio Performance
3. Business Strategy
4. Business Vision
5. System Evaluations
6. Strategic Alignments
7. Strategic Recommendations
1. Investment Redundancy Rules
2. Investment Requirements
1. Fitness Models
2. Risk Analysis
3. Computational Intelligence
4. Numerical Methods
5. Mathematical Models
6. Requirements Matrices

Figure 98: Investment Redundancy process Inputs, Outputs, and Tools & Techniques.

Resource Redundancy
1. Portfolio Valuation
2. Portfolio Performance
3. Business Strategy
4. Business Vision
5. System Evaluations
6. Strategic Alignments
7. Strategic Recommendations
1. Resource Redundancy Rules
2. Resource Requirements
1. Fitness Models
2. Risk Analysis
3. Computational Intelligence
4. Numerical Methods
5. Mathematical Models
6. Requirements Matrices

Figure 99: Resource Redundancy process Inputs, Outputs, and Tools & Techniques.

Investment Gap
1. Portfolio Valuation
2. Portfolio Performance
3. Business Strategy
4. Business Vision
5. System Evaluations
6. Strategic Alignments
7. Strategic Recommendations
1. Investment Gap Rules
2. Investment Requirements
1. Fitness Models
2. Risk Analysis
3. Computational Intelligence
4. Numerical Methods
5. Mathematical Models
6. Requirements Matrices

Figure 100: Investment Gap process Inputs, Outputs, and Tools & Techniques.

Resource Gap
1. Portfolio Valuation
2. Portfolio Performance
3. Business Strategy
4. Business Vision
5. System Evaluations
6. Strategic Alignments
7. Strategic Recommendations
1. Resource Gap Rules
2. Resource Requirements
1. Fitness Models
2. Risk Analysis
3. Computational Intelligence
4. Numerical Methods
5. Mathematical Models
6. Requirements Matrices

Figure 101: Resource Gap process Inputs, Outputs, and Tools & Techniques.

Investment Merger
1. Portfolio Valuation
2. Portfolio Performance
3. Business Strategy
4. Business Vision
5. System Evaluations
6. Strategic Alignments
7. Strategic Recommendations
1. Investment Merger Rules
2. Investment Requirements
1. Fitness Models
2. Risk Analysis
3. Computational Intelligence
4. Numerical Methods
5. Mathematical Models
6. Requirements Matrices

Figure 102: Investment Merger process Inputs, Outputs, and Tools & Techniques.

Resource Merger
1. Portfolio Valuation
2. Portfolio Performance
3. Business Strategy
4. Business Vision
5. System Evaluations
6. Strategic Alignments
7. Strategic Recommendations
1. Resource Merger Rules
2. Resource Requirements
1. Fitness Models
2. Risk Analysis
3. Computational Intelligence
4. Numerical Methods
5. Mathematical Models
6. Requirements Matrices

Figure 103: Resource Merger process Inputs, Outputs, and Tools & Techniques.

Investment Division
1. Portfolio Valuation
2. Portfolio Performance
3. Business Strategy
4. Business Vision
5. System Evaluations
6. Strategic Alignments
7. Strategic Recommendations
1. Investment Division Rules
2. Investment Requirements
1. Fitness Models
2. Risk Analysis
3. Computational Intelligence
4. Numerical Methods
5. Mathematical Models
6. Requirements Matrices

Figure 104: Investment Division process Inputs, Outputs, and Tools & Techniques.

Resource Division
1. Portfolio Valuation
2. Portfolio Performance
3. Business Strategy
4. Business Vision
5. System Evaluations
6. Strategic Alignments
7. Strategic Recommendations
1. Resource Division Rules
2. Resource Requirements
1. Fitness Models
2. Risk Analysis
3. Computational Intelligence
4. Numerical Methods
5. Mathematical Models
6. Requirements Matrices

Figure 105: Resource Division process Inputs, Outputs, and Tools & Techniques.

Rationalization Model

The Rationalization Model accumulates the information gathered on Redundancy, Gap, Obsolescence, Reuse, Merger, and Division and analyzes it further to formulate a model that is used to make rationalization decisions. The requirements, purpose, and functionality of the investments are analyzed along with IT architecture, investment performance, and capability. These inputs drive the formulation of the Rationalization Model.

Each of the processes in the Rationalization Model examines different aspects of the investments and proposes rules that may be used to identify rationalization targets. These proposed rules are inputs to the Rationalization Model Definition.

Requirements Analysis examines the investment requirements, purpose and functionality. This information is gathered in the Redundancy, Gap, Obsolescence, Reuse, Merger, and Division processes leading up to the Rationalization Model.

IT projects are particularly concerned with the software, database, deployment, and network architectures. Portfolios containing IT investments will want to examine these architecture concerns separately. These architecture concerns influence rationalization decisions and should be reflected in the model.

Performance Analysis examines the performance of the investments as they relate to the overall portfolio. The Rationalization Model may use these performance measures in determining rationalization decisions.

Capability Analysis examines the individual capabilities brought by each of the investments. The Rationalization Model may use this information to formulate decisions on which investments to rationalize and which to leave intact.

Finally, the Rationalization Model Definition process formalizes the Rationalization Model. This process examines all of the information brought to bear and creates a decision process that is used to determine which investments should be rationalized and which should be left. The Rationalization Model is this decision process. This may be as simple as a set of cutoff criteria where assets falling on one side of the cutoff are rationalized, or the process may be more complicated involving intelligent software systems and mathematical analysis.

Requirements Analysis

Requirements Analysis reviews and compiles the requirements, purpose and functionality of the investments in the portfolio. This information is gathered during the Redundancy, Gap, Obsolescence, Reuse, Merger, and Division processes. The Requirements Analysis process analyzes all of this information together in context to identify potential rules that may be incorporated into the Rationalization Model.

The Rationalization Manager determines the appropriate level of detail used in Requirements Analysis. Too much detail and the rationalization process may become mired in a sea of requirements without hope of understanding the overall picture. Too little detail and the model will not be able to identify rationalization targets because not enough information is present to make informed decisions. Part of the art of portfolio rationalization lies in the ability of the Rationalization Manager to choose the right amount of information to examine.

Requirements Analysis
1. Investment Requirements 2. Resource Requirements
1. Portfolio Requirements Rules
1. Fitness Models 2. Risk Analysis 3. Computational Intelligence 4. Numerical Methods 5. Mathematical Models 6. Requirements Matrices

Figure 106: Requirements Analysis process Inputs, Outputs, and Tools & Techniques.

Architecture Analysis
1. Investment Requirements 2. Resource Requirements
1. Architecture Rules
1. Fitness Models 2. Risk Analysis 3. Computational Intelligence 4. Numerical Methods 5. Mathematical Models 6. Requirements Matrices

Figure 107: Architecture Analysis process Inputs, Outputs, and Tools & Techniques.

Performance Analysis
1. Investment Requirements 2. Resource Requirements
1. Performance Rules
1. Fitness Models 2. Risk Analysis 3. Computational Intelligence 4. Numerical Methods 5. Mathematical Models 6. Requirements Matrices

Figure 108: Performance Analysis process Inputs, Outputs, and Tools & Techniques.

Compliance Analysis
1. Investment Requirements 2. Resource Requirements
1. Compliance Rules
1. Fitness Models 2. Risk Analysis 3. Computational Intelligence 4. Numerical Methods 5. Mathematical Models 6. Requirements Matrices

Figure 109: Compliance Analysis process Inputs, Outputs, and Tools & Techniques.

Capability Analysis
1. Investment Requirements 2. Resource Requirements
1. Capability Rules
1. Fitness Models 2. Risk Analysis 3. Computational Intelligence 4. Numerical Methods 5. Mathematical Models 6. Requirements Matrices

Figure 110: Capability Analysis process Inputs, Outputs, and Tools & Techniques.

Rationalization Model Deifinition
1. Investment Obsolescence Rules 2. Resource Obsolescence Rules 3. Investment Redundancy Rules 4. Resource Redundancy Rules 5. Investment Merger Rules 6. Resource Merger Rules 7. Investment Reuse Rules 8. Resource Reuse Rules 9. Investment Gap Rules 10. Resource Gap Rules 11. Investment Division Rules 12. Resource Division Rules 13. Portfolio Requirements Rules 14. Architecture Rules 15. Performance Rules 16. Capability Rules 17. Compliance Rules
1. Rationalization Model
1. Fitness Models 2. Risk Analysis 3. Computational Intelligence 4. Numerical Methods 5. Mathematical Models 6. Requirements Matrices

Figure 111: Rationalization Model Definition process Inputs, Outputs, and Tools & Techniques.

Architecture Analysis

Architecture Analysis is particular to IT portfolios. Architecture reviews to the structure and design of software, databases, networks, and deployment. IT architectures typically are designed to adhere to some set of design principles that are specific to the situation at hand. Because of these concerns, the system architectures should be examined for rationalization impacts.

Architecture impacts to rationalization come in two flavors. First, the architectures themselves may be targets for rationalization. In these cases the architectures are analyzed in the six surrounding processes. Second, rationalizing these architectures may have some unintended and undesirable consequences. In both cases, IT architectures should be handled carefully in the rationalization process.

Performance Analysis

Performance Analysis examines the contribution of each investment to the overall performance of the portfolio. It may be desirable to formulate rules for the Rationalization Model to rationalize underperforming investments. However, some investments have variable performance by nature. This year's underperformer may be next year's superstar.

Overall, performance may be a factor in the rationalization decision. If so, rationalization rules are proposed in this process that may be later incorporated into the Rationalization Model.

Compliance Analysis

Compliance is another contributor to the Rationalization Model. Compliance Analysis develops potential rules to identify rationalization targets based on compliance criteria. This process is performed in a similar fashion to the previous processes but with a focus on compliance issues.

Capability Analysis

Investment capability is another factor that may be incorporated into the Rationalization Model. Capability Analysis examines the various capabilities brought by the investments to the portfolio. Similar to the previous processes, rules may be proposed to identify rationalization targets based on their capabilities.

Capability Analysis is particularly concerned with gaps and redundancies. Redundant capabilities may provide rationalization targets. However, gaps may indicate areas where additional capabilities may be useful. This process can identify areas of expansion of the business as opportunities to provide products and services previously overlooked.

Rationalization Model Definition

Rationalization Model Definition formalizes the rules used to identify rationalization targets. These rules form a decision process which is the Rationalization Model. The other processes in Rationalization Model Analysis propose rules addressing a particular aspect of interest. Rationalization Model Definition examines each of these rules and may accept, reject, or combine rules. Furthermore, this process may formulate entirely new rules to accommodate situations that were not anticipated from examining individual investment aspects.

Each process in the Rationalization Model analyzes a different investment aspect and formulates decision rules that may be incorporated into the Rationalization Model. These processes identify key measures, examine the investments, and formulate potential rules. The Rationalization Model Definition combines these results to create the overall rationalization rule set which is the Rationalization Model.

The Rationalization Model is the key model of the Portfolio Rationalization Process. It is this model that identifies specific investments as targets for rationalization. These rationalization targets are the output of the Rationalization Selection process and are put into the Transformation Plan.

10 Introducing Rationalization to the Organization

Introducing portfolio rationalization to an organization is a process unto itself. Essentially, we need to examine the strategy and vision of the organization to tailor a process suitable to obtain the desired Portfolio Performance. In addition, we need to identify the method used to obtain fundamental information such as Asset Information and System Requirements.

We need to be careful to not overcomplicate the procedure during the early formulation of the Portfolio Rationalization Process. It is tempting for Portfolio Managers to create elaborate processes with many detailed parts in order to achieve optimal results. However, when first starting portfolio rationalization, it is recommended that the process be implemented as a series of small well-defined procedures. This allows the participants and the organization an opportunity to adjust to the new process and see the benefits. Large, sweeping changes to an established organization may be met with negative sentiments and the process may not be given an opportunity to demonstrate utility.

Although there may be no well defined process in place, this does not mean that a legacy process does not already exist. Many times portfolio rationalization is performed by Portfolio Managers and Executives without a well structured process. However, it's likely there are already certain practices in place, and the organization may have expectations that similar procedures will continue in the future. Legacy procedures such as these should be incorporated into the Portfolio Rationalization Process whenever they add value.

Figure 112 presents the process flow for Portfolio Rationalization Setup. The process begins by Evaluating Strategy & Value in order to obtain the Business Strategy and Vision. This information is used to Identify Statutes and Regulations applicable to the portfolio under consideration. The Business Strategy, Vision, and the Statutes and Regulations are used to assess organizational needs for rationalization. Based on this, we create a business case for implementing a Portfolio Rationalization Process.

The business case is reviewed and approved by an Executive sponsor. Once approved, we can begin defining the elements necessary for the rationalization process. We identify the specific investments that make up the portfolio. In addition, we formulate the Performance Expectations of the portfolio. From the identified investments, we can create the Asset Information Procedure. These are all external inputs to the Portfolio Rationalization Process.

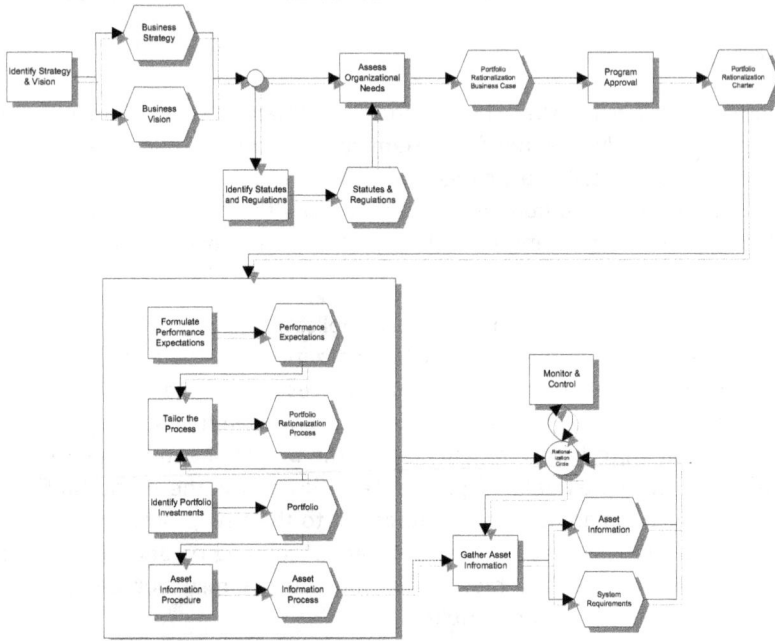

Figure 112: Portfolio Rationalization Setup process flow.

With these framework elements in place, we can begin the Portfolio Rationalization Process. However, we need to gather Asset Information for the Portfolio Snapshot and obtain System Requirements during the process execution. The Portfolio Rationalization Process can reach back to this initial setup process to get this information when needed. Finally, we have an external Monitor & Control process that observes the Portfolio Rationalization Process and updates the process as required.

Identify Strategy & Vision

Identify Strategy & Vision identifies the Business Strategy and Business Vision documentation. Organizations typically have these documents prepared, but often the Business Vision is a part of the Business Strategy document.

If these documents are not prepared, then a preliminary document should be created. The Vision and Strategy provide the organizational direction and the Portfolio Performance is measured according to this strategy.

Identify Strategy & Vision
1. Business Strategy 2. Business Vision
1. Interviews 2. Questionnaires

Identify Statutes and Regulations
1. Business Strategy 2. Business Vision
1. Statutes & Regulations 2. Legal Opinion
1. Legal Research

Assess Organizational Needs
1. Business Strategy 2. Business Vision
1. Portfolio Rationalization Business Case
1. Interviews 2. Questionnaires

Figure 113: Identify Strategy & Vision process Inputs, Outputs, and Tools & Techniques.

Figure 114: Identify Statutes and Regulations process Inputs, Outputs, and Tools & Techniques.

Figure 115: Assess Organizational Needs process Inputs, Outputs, and Tools & Techniques.

Identify Statutes and Regulations

Identify Statutes and Regulations determines how the portfolio is affected by Federal, State, and Local laws. Many portfolios are not affected by laws in any way. In these cases, this process may be skipped.

There are some portfolios which are heavily influenced by laws and regulations. In these cases, this process is used to better understand these laws and determine what affect the laws may have on the portfolio investments. This process aims to interpret these laws and provide insight to the goals of the portfolio.

Interpreting laws and regulations is a complete process that requires specialized legal training. Lawyers with knowledge in these areas should be consulted to do the legal research necessary to identify which laws are applicable.

In addition, a Legal Opinion may also be required. A Legal Opinion is prepared by an attorney and states how the statutes and regulations are interpreted by the courts and what the organization needs to do in order to comply. The Legal Opinion provides guidance on what needs to be done with the portfolio investments to attain or maintain regulatory and statutory compliance.

Assess Organizational Needs

This process uses the Business Strategy, Business Vision, Statutes & Regulations, and Legal Opinions to create a business case for implementing Portfolio Rationalization. This is a go/no-go phase gate in the Portfolio Rationalization Setup process.

The Business Case should examine the needs of the organization in light of the current investments to determine if Portfolio Rationalization adds value. Small portfolios and/or small organizations may not be able to receive a net benefit from the Portfolio Rationalization Process. It may be the case that the cost of implementing the rationalization process actually exceeds the potential value.

The Business Case should also identify an overall purpose for the portfolio and a potential set of investments under consideration. These investments are candidates for the portfolio but are not necessarily part of the portfolio. Final decision on the portfolio investments occurs later in the Identify Portfolio Investments process.

The Business Case should examine these factors and make recommendations for proceeding or not proceeding with the implementation of a Portfolio Rationalization Process. In either case, the results should be documented and sent to Executive leadership for consideration and review.

Program Approval
1. Portfolio Rationalization Business Case
1. Portfolio Rationalization Charter

Identify Portfolio Investments
1. Business Strategy
2. Business Vision
3. Statutes & Regulations
1. Process Updates
1. Corrective Actions

Formulate Performance Expectations
1. Business Strategy
2. Business Vision
3. Statutes and Regulations
1. Performance Expectations
1. Interviews
2. Questionnaires

Figure 116: Program Approval process Inputs, Outputs, and Tools & Techniques.

Figure 117: Identify Portfolio Investments process Inputs, Outputs, and Tools & Techniques.

Figure 118: Formulate Performance Expectations process Inputs, Outputs, and Tools & Techniques.

Program Approval

Executive leaders then review the Business Case presented and decide if there is sufficient justification to proceed with the implementation of a Portfolio Rationalization Process. Formal approval comes in the form of a Program Charter.

Identify Portfolio Investments

Once Portfolio Rationalization is formally approved, we can start a more detailed investigation of candidates for investments for the portfolio. As there may be a wide range of investments, it is usually better to first obtain permission to move forward with the Portfolio Rationalization Process before starting a detailed investigation of investments for the portfolio.

The appropriate investments for the portfolio are chosen while accounting for the Business Strategy, Business Vision, Statutes & Regulations, Legal Opinions, and recommendations from the Executives approving the Program Charter. The investments do not need to have a single coherent purpose. Investments may be grouped together simply for convenience. However, portfolios with a unified purpose are preferred.

The final selection of investments for the portfolio should be reviewed and approved by Executive leadership. This will help to reduce conflicts between Portfolio Managers and will help to assure that investments are not analyzed through multiple Portfolio Rationalization Processes.

Formulate Performance Expectations

Performance Expectations for the portfolio are an input to the Portfolio Rationalization Process. Some portfolios may be able to have these expectations specified before we have picked the investments. Portfolios for regulatory compliance may be able to set expectations without considering the underlying investments.

In other cases we may need to first identify the portfolio investments before we can specify the Performance Expectations. Performance Expectations may be set as a relative improvement in total performance of the group of investments. In these cases we first need to know what the investments are so we can determine the present performance, then set expectations for the future.

In any case, the output of this process is some set of Performance Expectations for the portfolio. The rationalization process will evaluate the performance of the portfolio against these expectations and identify opportunities for improvements based on the information specified in this process.

Asset Information Procedure

The Asset Information Procedure process specifies how Asset Information and System Requirements are identified. Asset Information is essential for the Portfolio Snapshot, and System Requirements are a critical input to the Rationalization Model.

Here we examine the sources of data (people, documents, databases, data warehouses, etc.), and determine the best process for gathering the necessary information. The recommended process may differ depending on what information we need and when we need it.

The Asset Information Procedure document specifies how we plan to gather the information needed for the Portfolio Rationalization Process. This document includes a list of stakeholders, communications requirements, available data, the preferred methods of obtaining the data, alternative methods of obtaining data, and any other factors that should be considered when requesting data for an investment.

Asset Information Procedure
1. Business Strategy 2. Business Vision 3. Statutes and Regulations
1. Asset Information Process
1. Interviews 2. Questionnaires

Tailor the Process
1. Business Strategy 2. Business Vision 3. Statutes and Regulations 4. Performance Expectations 5. Asset Information Process
1. Portfolio Rationalization Process
1. Interviews 2. Questionnaires

Figure 119: Asset Information Procedure process Inputs, Outputs, and Tools & Techniques.

Figure 120: Tailor the Process Inputs, Outputs, and Tools & Techniques.

Tailor the Process

Tailor the Process identifies the processes and techniques that are implemented in the Portfolio Rationalization Process. This process examines the Business Strategy, Business Vision, Statutes and Regulations, Legal Opinions, Performance Expectations, and Asset Information Procedures to determine which processes are good candidates for inclusion and which should be left out for the moment.

An initial Portfolio Rationalization Process should be as simple as possible while achieving the organizational objectives. This provides an opportunity for the users and Executives to evaluate the process and see the benefits that the process provides.

Overly complex processes may be detrimental in the early implementation of Portfolio Rationalization. Users may see the processes as difficult to understand and interrupting the way they do their jobs. Executives may see complex processes as costly and not returning value in proportion to the cost of maintaining the processes.

For these reasons it is recommended that initial Portfolio Rationalization implementations use only a few processes that immediately add value rather than attempting to apply a full-blown Portfolio Rationalization. In addition, initial implementations should focus on producing immediate and identifiable returns to the organization as opposed to spending significant time and effort on creating a fully automated rationalization process.

Gather Asset Information
1. Asset Information Process
1. Asset Information 2. System Requirements
1. Data Repositories 2. Status Reports 3. Field Investigations 4. Interviews 5. Questionnaires

Monitor & Control
1. Process Performance
1. Process Updates
1. Corrective Actions

Figure 121: Gather Asset Information process Inputs, Outputs, and Tools & Techniques.

Figure 122: Monitor & Control process Inputs, Outputs, and Tools & Techniques.

Gather Asset Information

The Gather Asset Information process implements all or part of the Asset Information Procedure to obtain a specific set of data. This is required for the Portfolio Snapshot and during the formulation of the Rationalization Model.

The process of gathering the data is executed according to the process specified in the Asset Information Procedure. This document details the various information available, stakeholder contact information, and how to obtain updates.

This process is loosely coupled to the Portfolio Rationalization Process even though it is external to the rationalization process. The rationalization process may need to regularly call back to this process for new information, updates, or additional detail.

Monitor & Control

Monitor & Control functions as quality assurance and quality control for the Portfolio Rationalization Process. Any of the Portfolio Rationalization Processes or models can be subject to review by a monitor/control process.

There are two main goals for Monitor and Control: 1) Assure the process is running to specifications and 2) Identify opportunities to enhance the process. The first goal may be achieved via standard quality assurance and quality control procedures. The second goal requires the evaluation of the process by the Rationalization Manager to identify opportunities for process improvement, automation, or tuning.

11 Advanced Tools and Techniques

This section discusses some more advanced tools and techniques used in portfolio rationalization. Many rationalization efforts do not use any of these advanced tools. However, the tools are extremely beneficial in certain cases.

It is not necessary to fully understand these concepts in order to use the Portfolio Rationalization Process. The process may be implemented without using any of these advanced concepts. However, a fully automated process will likely wish to make use of some of these concepts in order to automate the process to its full extent.

Computational Intelligence

Computational Intelligence is a computer science discipline directed toward the construction of intelligent computer systems. Computational Intelligence uses several automated optimization techniques that may be beneficial to the portfolio rationalization analysis.

Computational Intelligence specializes in feedback learning systems. These systems acquire new data and modify themselves based on this new information. Learning systems like these may be useful when automating the Portfolio Rationalization Process.

Evolutionary Computing

Evolutionary Computing uses an iterative procedure to evolve some system in response to new information. Typically, these systems are used to solve combinatorial optimization problems. These are particularly difficult problems and are usually approached with specialized techniques.

As a simple example, we may want to find the maximum of some function $f(x)$. We could just test random points and track the lowest value. This brute force approach might eventually come up with the correct answer, but it will probably take a long time to find a value close to the optimum.

Alternatively, an evolutionary computing approach might take several samples of $f(x)$ at different values of x, then use this collective information to determine good values of x to test. These new values form the next generation, and the process is iterated.

Genetic Algorithms

Genetic Algorithms are optimization algorithms modeled on the DNA reproduction/replication. In computer terms, the DNA represents some system state (the value of x to test). This process attempts to capture the evolutionary improvement aspects of how organisms evolve as a species.

We begin by taking some initial set of different states (start with 50 random values of x). Then we test the fitness of each (compute $f(x)$ for each of our 50 values of x). Next, we randomly select pairs from the set in proportion to their fitness (randomly choose two of the x's we have, but bias the selection in favor of the x's with high values of $f(x)$).

Then we perform a crossover or mutation. For a crossover, we swap and combine parts of the DNA strands to form two new strands. We repeat until we have the desired number of states for the next generation (repeat until we have 50 new x's). Then iterate the entire process. For mutation, we randomly choose some part(s) of a DNA strand and modify it at that point.

The steps in the process are:

1. **Identify a fitness function f** - The fitness function is an essential ingredient for Genetic Algorithms. The analysis works with experts to identify a fitness function that captures the optimization desires of the customer.
2. **Create a genetic representation of the problem space** – This is a computer representation of the possible solutions to the problem. In the above example, this would be the values of x and the genetic representation might be the bit representation of x in the computer memory.
3. **Select some initial states** – Initial states are chosen at random, however, if there is some set of known good starting points, this can be used instead.
4. **Test each state with the fitness function** - Evaluate f for each x.
5. **Select one or more states biased by their fitness** – There are many possible methods that can be used to produce a biased selection. However, using a weighted random number generator (see Random Number Generation) is a particularly useful method.
6. **Modify the selected state(s) to generate a new state** – There are two main methods used to generate new states: Crossover and Mutation. These may be used by themselves or separately.

i. <u>Crossover</u> – Start with two states x_1 and x_2. Choose a point within the states. Swap part of x_1 with the opposite part of x_2. Generate another state by combining the other part of x_1 with x_2.

ii. <u>Mutation</u> – Start with a single state. Pick a point within the state. Randomly change the value of this part to another acceptable value.

7. **Repeat** 5 until the desired number of states is reached.

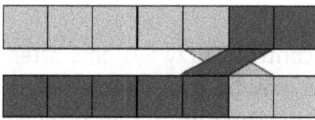

8. **Return** to step 4.

Figure 123: Crossover between two states.   Figure 124: Mutation of a state.

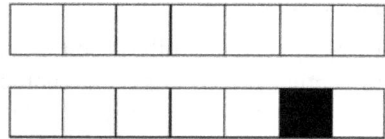

This basic process often converges quickly on optimal solutions. Moreover, the process is fairly simple to implement in software systems.

There are many variations to this process. It should be noted that Genetic Algorithms can be based entirely on mutation with no crossover whatsoever. This may be an effective technique when working with systems where two different states cannot necessarily be represented with a uniform genetic representation.

Genetic Programming

Genetic Programming is a method of constructing computer based programs that use Genetic Algorithms to find an optimal program structure. This field includes evolvable hardware solutions, quantum computing, and evolutionary game strategy.

In a sense, Genetic Programs are the application of Genetic Algorithms to programming. However, Genetic Programs often have an external source of feedback. This allows Genetic Programs to evolve their behavior in response to external stimuli, whereas Genetic Algorithms typically only seek a solution to a specific, fixed problem.

A simple example of a Genetic Program might be a product shipping application. Imagine we sell some product, and have several shipping carriers that we can use. When a customer places an order, we need to select a particular carrier. In addition, suppose our customers give us feedback about shipping.

Initially, we just randomly choose a carrier and start receiving some feedback from our customers. At this point we can use the feedback as a fitness function for a Genetic Program. On future orders, the program selects a carrier randomly, but biased by their fitness.

As we continue to fill orders, a preferred carrier may lose favor with our customers. This will be reflected as a drop in the fitness score for the carrier, and the program will automatically respond by decreasing the frequency that carrier is selected. In this manner, the Genetic Program actively evolves in response to the dynamic customer preferences.

Fuzzy Systems

Fuzzy Systems are often used in machine control. Fuzzy Systems attempt to capture the concept that characteristics may be overlapping (warm v. hot). Elements do not strictly fall into a specific set; rather, they can have a partial membership in multiple sets.

These control systems may be used effectively in cases where there is a concept of partial membership. For example, an asset may be characterized as in or out of compliance. However, in many cases, an asset may be very close to compliant while another asset may be completely incompliant. In cases such as these, Fuzzy Systems may be used to express the near-compliance of one system versus the complete incompliance of another system.

Artificial Neural Networks

Artificial Neural Networks (ANNs) are computer simulations of the behavior of axons and dendrites in physiological brains. Conceptually, ANNs are a system of nodes. These nodes are connected to other nodes in the system. Information flows into the nodes from sources (other nodes or inputs), is processed at the node, and then is outputted from the node.

Recurrent networks are networks where the nodes are connected together to form loops where the output of one node feeds a second node, and the second node is an input to the first. These networks can demonstrate chaotic behavior as nodes receive inputs, process the inputs, and then create outputs which in turn affect their own inputs.

Non-Recurrent networks do not allow these looping connections. Non-Recurrent networks only flow information in one direction. These are called Feed-forward networks. Feed-forward networks are stable and do not demonstrate chaotic behavior.

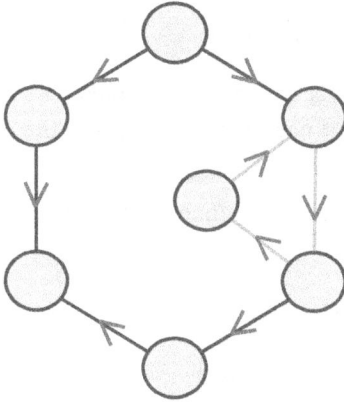

Figure 125: Recurrent network indicating the area of recurrence.

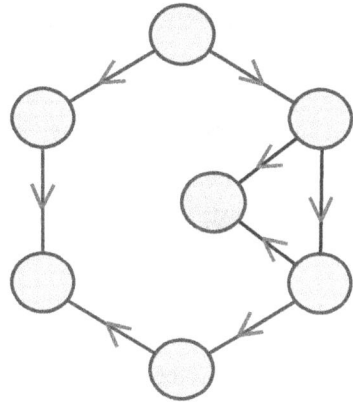

Figure 126: Feed-forward (Non-recurrent) network.

ANNs designate nodes as inputs, outputs, or hidden. Input nodes are nodes that are initially set with an input pattern. Output nodes are nodes that define the results of the ANN. Hidden nodes are used for processing, but are not part of the inputs or outputs.

ANNs are typically used for some type of pattern recognition. Pattern recognition is the problem of examining some input and associating it with a particular output. For example, the XOR function is a binary function that associates binary input patterns to a single output: $(1,1) -> 0$, $(1,0) -> 1$, $(0,1) -> 1$, $(0,0) -> 0$. In this sense many functions are types of pattern-matching problems.

Backpropagation

Backpropagation is a technique for creating an ANN. First, we identify some set of inputs and outputs that we want to match. In general, each input is a vector in i-dimensions, while the output is a vector in k-dimensions.

In addition to the inputs and outputs, we have some hidden nodes. These nodes are typically setup as a series of layers. The inputs feed the first hidden layer. The first hidden layer feeds the second hidden layer. The second hidden layer feeds the third, etc. Finally, the last hidden layer feeds the output layer.

The output of any given node is determined by computing the weighted sum of the nodes' inputs, adding a threshold, and applying an activation function. Mathematically,

$$N_\beta^l = A\left(\tau_\beta + \sum \omega_{\alpha\beta} H_\alpha{}^{l-1}\right)$$

11-1

where N_β^l is the output of the β node in layer l, τ_β is the threshold for the node, and $\omega_{\alpha\beta}$ is the weight between the α node in layer $l-1$ and the β node in layer l.

A typical activation function used in backpropagation is the sigmoid function

$$A(x) = \frac{1}{1 + e^{-x}}$$

11-2

This function is used because it resembles an on-off switch. At the extreme limits $\lim_{x \to -1} A(x) \to 0$ and $\lim_{x \to 1} A(x) \to 1$. Near $x = 0$ the function rises from 0 and moves toward 1.

The backpropagation technique allows us to compute the best-fit values for τ_β and $\omega_{\alpha\beta}$. The technique examines the squared-error of the ANN output relative to the desired output, summed for every input-output pair. From this, we use the steepest descents algorithm to iteratively update the values for τ_β and $\omega_{\alpha\beta}$ until an optimum is reached.

Assume we have N total input-output vector pairs. Let I_{in} be the nth input vector and O_{kn} be the corresponding output vector. Assume there is only one hidden layer, with the layer containing h total hidden nodes. Let A_k^O be the activation function of the kth output node and A_j^H be the activation function of the jth hidden node. Let τ_k be the threshold for the kth output and ω_{jk} be the weight between the jth hidden node and k^{th} output node. Furthermore, let $\bar{\tau}_j$ be the threshold for the jth hidden node and $\bar{\omega}_{ij}$ be the weight between the ith input and j^{th} hidden node

The output of the output nodes is given by

$$O_k = A_k^O\left(\tau_k + \sum_j \omega_{jk} H_j\right)$$

11-3

where H_j is the output of the hidden nodes,

$$H_j = A_j^H\left(\bar{\tau}_j + \sum_j \bar{\omega}_{ij} I_i\right)$$

11-4

From these formulas we can see how to start with a set of input values I_i, use them to compute the hidden values H_j, then use these to compute the output values O_k.

Now, given some set of input-output pairs, we want to find the values for τ_k, ω_{jk}, $\bar{\tau}_j$, and $\bar{\omega}_{ij}$ that best fit the data to this model. To accomplish this, we define the square distance between the current output values and the desired values. The measured inputs are I_{in} with corresponding outputs O_{kn}. The squared distance is

$$\chi^2 = \frac{1}{2}\sum_n (O_k - O_{kn})^2$$

11-5

where the factor of ½ is for later convenience.

We want to optimize this with respect to the full set of parameters. In order to do this, we use the gradient descent method to iteratively converge on the optimum parameter values.

We start with some initial set of parameter values. To find the optimum value for one of the parameters, we take the partial derivative with respect to the parameter and decrease the factor in proportion,

$$\theta^{new} = \theta^{previous} - \delta\frac{\partial\chi^2}{\partial\theta}$$

11-6

where δ is a predetermined constant less than 1. We complete this calculation for every parameter. Then we iterate the entire process.

Thus, we need to compute this partial derivative for each of the four parameter types.

$$\frac{\partial\chi^2}{\partial\tau_k} = A_k^{O'}\left(\tau_k + \sum_j \omega_{jk} H_j\right)$$

11-7

$$\frac{\partial\chi^2}{\partial\omega_{jk}} = A_k^{O'}\left(\tau_k + \sum_j \omega_{jk} H_j\right)H_j$$

11-8

$$\frac{\partial\chi^2}{\partial\bar{\tau}_j} = A_k^{O'}\left(\tau_k + \sum_j \omega_{jk} H_j\right)\omega_{jk}\frac{\partial H_j}{\partial\bar{\tau}_j}$$

11-9

$$= \omega_{jk} A_k^{O'}\left(\tau_k + \sum_j \omega_{jk} H_j\right)A_j^{H'}\left(\bar{\tau}_j + \sum_j \bar{\omega}_{ij} I_i\right)$$

11-10

$$\frac{\partial\chi^2}{\partial\bar{\omega}_{ij}} = A_k^{O'}\left(\tau_k + \sum_j \omega_{jk} H_j\right)\omega_{jk}\frac{\partial H_j}{\partial\bar{\omega}_{ij}}$$

11-11

$$= \omega_{jk} A_k^{O'} \left(\tau_k + \sum_j \omega_{jk} H_j \right) A_j^{H'} \left(\bar{\tau}_j + \sum_j \bar{\omega}_{ij} I_i \right) I_i \qquad \text{11-12}$$

Thus, the updates for the parameters is

$$\Delta \tau_k = -\delta A_k^{O'} \left(\tau_k + \sum_j \omega_{jk} H_j \right) \qquad \text{11-13}$$

$$\Delta \omega_{jk} = -\delta A_k^{O'} \left(\tau_k + \sum_j \omega_{jk} H_j \right) H_j \qquad \text{11-14}$$

$$\Delta \bar{\tau}_j = -\delta \omega_{jk} A_k^{O'} \left(\tau_k + \sum_j \omega_{jk} H_j \right) A_j^{H'} \left(\bar{\tau}_j + \sum_j \bar{\omega}_{ij} I_i \right) \qquad \text{11-15}$$

$$\Delta \bar{\omega}_{ij} = -\delta \omega_{jk} A_k^{O'} \left(\tau_k + \sum_j \omega_{jk} H_j \right) A_j^{H'} \left(\bar{\tau}_j + \sum_j \bar{\omega}_{ij} I_i \right) I_i \qquad \text{11-16}$$

With these, we can specify the process for creating the neural network.

1. Identify a set of input-output pairs we want to model
2. Choose the number of hidden neurons
3. Choose an activation function for each of the hidden and output neurons
4. Randomly set all of the parameter values
5. For every input we want to model
    a. Place the input values into the network
    b. Compute the values of the hidden nodes
    c. Compute the values of the output nodes
    d. Compute the squared distance between the output values from the network and the desired output
6. Use the parameter adjustment equations to adjust the network parameters
7. Return to step 5

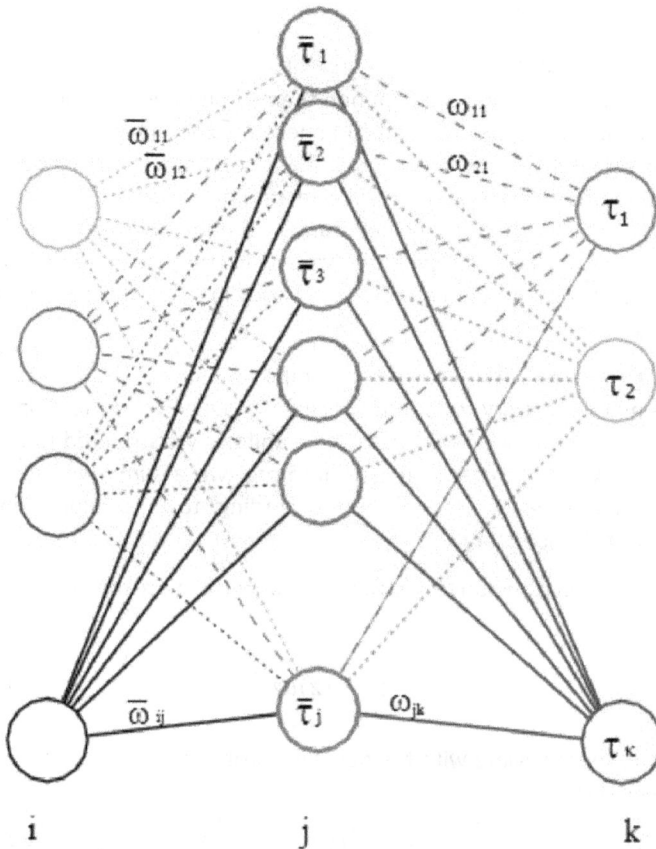

Figure 127: Structure of an artificial neural network showing the weight connections and node thresholds.

Numerical Analysis

Numerical analysis uses computations to approximate or model a system. Typically, numerical analysis uses a computer program to compute values for the system and attempt to evolve the system over time. This is useful in portfolio rationalization as a means to predict how an investment or group of investments may behave over time. This is particularly useful when analyzing how different factors might affect the future values of the investments.

Many of these calculations rely on a few mathematical concepts. In this section, we introduce some of these concepts. However, there are many great treatises for each of these concepts in the literature, and the reader is directed to the bibliography to gain a deeper understanding of how to utilize these techniques.

Random Number Generation

Random number generation is a common theme in numerical analysis. We have already encountered the need to generate biased random numbers when we discussed Genetic Algorithms. Most software implementations have some method of generating uniform random numbers. These are random numbers on some specified range. The number generated is randomly selected from all possible values in the given range. The generation of uniform random numbers is a study in itself which we do not discuss here.

Our task is to take a uniformly distributed random number and generate a random number according to some specified probability distribution. To begin, we assume that we have access to a uniformly distributed random deviate which we designate as u. Furthermore, we assume we wish to create a random deviate distributed according to a predetermined probability distribution $D(x)$.

First, compute the cumulative distribution function from the probability density

$$C(x) = \int_{-\infty}^{x} D(z)dz \qquad \text{11-17}$$

Formally, a random deviate with the desired distribution is computed from the uniform deviate as

$$\rho = C^{-1}(u) \qquad \text{11-18}$$

where u is the uniform deviate on the range $[0,1)$, C^{-1} is the inverse of the cumulative distribution function, and ρ is a random deviate distributed according to the probability distribution $D(x)$.

This process may be best demonstrated with a concrete example. Suppose we want to compute a random deviate according to the exponential probability distribution

$$D(x) = \begin{cases} \alpha e^{-\alpha x} & x \geq 0 \\ 0 & x < 0 \end{cases} \qquad \text{11-19}$$

The cumulative distribution function is

$$C(x) = \int_{-\infty}^{x} D(z)dz \qquad \text{11-20}$$

If $x < 0$, we have

$$C(x) = \int_{-\infty}^{x} D(z)dz = \int_{-\infty}^{x} 0\,dz = 0 \qquad \text{11-21}$$

If $x \geq 0$,

$$C(x) = \int_{-\infty}^{x} D(z)dz \qquad \text{11-22}$$

$$= \int_{-\infty}^{0} D(z)dz + \int_{0}^{x} D(z)dz \qquad \text{11-23}$$

$$= \int_{-\infty}^{0} 0\,dz + \int_{0}^{x} \alpha e^{-\alpha z}\,dz \qquad \text{11-24}$$

$$= \alpha \int_{0}^{x} e^{-\alpha z}\,dz \qquad \text{11-25}$$

$$= -e^{-\alpha z}\,|_{0}^{x} \qquad \text{11-26}$$

$$= 1 - e^{-\alpha x} \qquad \text{11-27}$$

We find the inverse of this by solving for x,

$$t = 1 - e^{-\alpha x} \qquad \text{11-28}$$

$$e^{-\alpha x} = 1 - t \qquad \text{11-29}$$

$$-\alpha x = ln(1 - t) \qquad \text{11-30}$$

$$x = -\frac{1}{\alpha}ln(1 - t) \qquad \text{11-31}$$

This is the expression for C^{-1},

$$C^{-1}(t) = -\frac{1}{\alpha}ln(1 - t) \qquad \text{11-32}$$

Substituting this into 11-18,

$$\rho = -\frac{1}{\alpha}ln(1 - u) \qquad \text{11-33}$$

If we start with a uniform deviate u and substitute it into the above expression, the result is a new deviate which is distributed according to the exponential distribution.

This technique is extremely useful when we need to generate a non-uniform (biased) random variable. The table below presents some probability density functions and the method of generating random deviates from uniform deviates. (Note: Expressions referring to u_1 and u_2 require two uniform deviates.)

Simulation

Numerical analysis is also used to simulate the behavior, interaction, and evolution of a system. Numerical analysis can vary parameters and evaluate specific scenarios to observe what possible results may occur in specific situations.

Probability Distribution   Generation

$$\text{Exponential: } E(x) = \begin{cases} ae^{-ax} & x \geq 0 \\ 0 & x < 0 \end{cases} \qquad \rho = -\frac{1}{a}\ln(1-u)$$

$$\text{Gaussian: } N(x) = \frac{1}{\sigma\sqrt{2\pi}}e^{-\frac{1}{2}\left(\frac{x}{\sigma}\right)^2} \qquad \rho = \sigma\sqrt{-2\ln u_1}\,\sin(2\pi u_2)$$

$$\text{Cauchy: } C(x) = \frac{1}{\pi\gamma\left[1+\left(\frac{x}{\gamma}\right)^2\right]} \qquad \rho = \frac{1}{2}+\frac{1}{\pi}\arctan\left(\frac{x}{\gamma}\right)$$

$$\text{Pareto: } P(x) = \frac{ka^k}{x^{k+1}} \qquad \rho = \frac{a}{\sqrt[k]{1-x}}$$

Monte Carlo Analysis

Monte Carlo Analysis is a type of simulation where random numbers are generated and used to aid in the simulation of events. The process is repeated to determine the probability an extent or outcome may occur.

As a simple example, we can compute the value of pi using Monte Carlo techniques. Begin with the unit square defined as the region $0 \leq x \leq 1$, $0 \leq y \leq 1$. Inscribe a circle inside the square. Perform the following sequence of steps:

1. Generate uniform deviates u_x and u_y.
2. If the point (u_x, u_y) lies inside the circle, add one to the Circle Count (C).
3. Execute this process a total of N times.

The frequency that a random point lays inside the circle is given by the ratio of the area of the circle to the area of the square. Since the square has length 1 on both sides, its area is simply 1. The circle has diameter 1 or radius ½. The area of the circle is $\pi r^2 = \frac{\pi}{4}$.

The ratio of the area of the circle to the area of the square is $\frac{\pi}{4}$. From this, we have

$$\frac{C}{N} \approx \frac{\pi}{4} \qquad \text{11-34}$$

or,

$$\pi \approx 4\frac{C}{N} \qquad \text{11-35}$$

The more we repeat the process, the more accurate the expression will become.

Stochastic Analysis

A Stochastic Process is a random process that evolves with time. Stochastic Processes may be used to model time varying systems that have a random component.

One example is the movement of the price of a stock over time. We can analyze the day-to-day variations and estimate a mean and standard deviation for the price movements. Based on this we can create sample price movements over a specified period of time.

These prices may be an input to another Numerical Analysis or Monte Carlo simulation. For example, we may have a portfolio asset whose monthly cost is dependent on the price of gasoline. We might model gas prices as a Stochastic Process, and then simulate several situations to see how sensitive the overall cost of the investment depends on the fluctuations in the price of gas.

Creating a sample stochastic process is fairly simple. Suppose we want to model a commodity where the day-to-day price change is fit to a normal distribution with mean μ and standard deviation σ. We would begin by compiling some historical data, then using a Regression Analysis to determine the best μ and σ to fit the historical data.

In order to compute a potential price movement over a period of days, we begin with an initial price P_0. Then we add a Gaussian distributed random deviate to this to get the price at day 1,

$$P_1 = P_0 + \rho_1 \qquad \text{11-36}$$

where ρ_1 is a Gaussian distributed random deviate. We continue the process iteratively,

$$P_2 = P_1 + \rho_2 \qquad \text{11-37}$$
$$\vdots$$
$$P_n = P_{n-1} + \rho_n$$

We can continue this process to obtain arbitrarily long sequences of prices. A process generated in this manner is called a Weiner process, or Brownian motion.

This process produces values at specific time increments. We may need to get values that lay in-between two consecutive points. It is not readily apparent how we can compute in-between values. Since we have the values at each endpoint, we need to compute random deviates that are distributed in such a way to account for both the initial and final values.

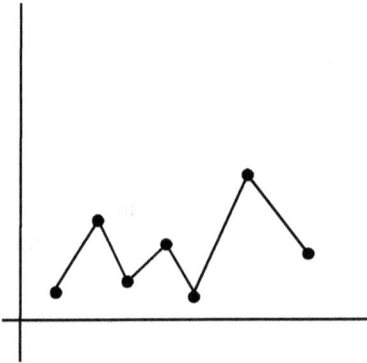

Figure 128: Example stochastic process.

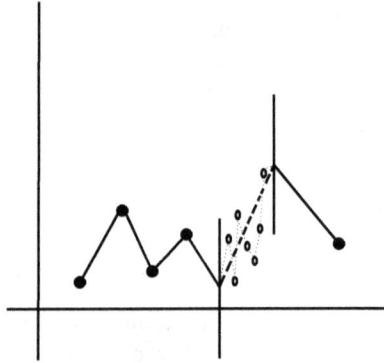

Figure 129: Interpolation between points in a stochastic process.

Based on this technique, we may obtain a set of discrete sample points on a continuous Brownian motion by selecting an interval s, then generating N random variables X_n where the random variables have a Normal distribution $N(0, \bar{\sigma}^2 s)$ (mean is 0, standard is $\bar{\sigma}^2 s$). The initial Brownian motion may be formed from partial sums of the random variables

$$B_n = \sum_{i=1}^{n} X_i \qquad \text{11-38}$$

The motion may be extended to longer times by generating additional random variables and extending the partial sums. However, we have no information on the points between these initial points.

First, it should be noted that we cannot generate a new random variable and simply insert it into the sum. For example, if we already know the value of the partial sums at points x and $x + s$ is B_x, B_{x+s}, it is tempting to generate a random variable with distribution $N(0, \bar{\sigma}^2 s/2)$, add this to B_x. This value does have the proper distribution with respect to x, however, there is no guarantee that we have the proper distribution with respect to $x + s$.

We wish to interpolate a value for the process between x and $x + s$ that has the proper distribution with respect to both B_x and B_{x+s}. With no loss in generality, set $B_x = x = 0$. We desire the probability density function for the random variable $0 < t < s$ given $B_0 = 0$ and $B_s = S$.

Because the Wiener process has stationary independent increments with normal distribution, we can conceive of the process as formed from two random variables. The first has value Δ_t and occurs at time t. The second has value Δ_s and occurs at time s. From the definition of the Wiener process, the joint density function of these variables is

$$f_{\Delta_t \Delta_s}(\delta_t, \delta_s) = N(\delta_t; 0, \sigma_t^2) N(\delta_s; 0, \sigma_s^2)$$

11-39

$$= \frac{1}{2\pi \sigma_t \sigma_s} e^{-\left(\frac{\delta_t^2}{2\sigma_t^2} + \frac{\delta_s^2}{2\sigma_s^2}\right)}$$

11-40

We know $B_s = S$ so $\delta_t + \delta_s = S$.

We want the conditional probability density $f_{\Delta_t | \Delta_t + \Delta_s = S}(\delta_t | \delta_t + \delta_s = S)$.

First, make a change of variables where
$$\begin{aligned} Z &= \Delta_t + \Delta_s \\ W &= \Delta_t \end{aligned}$$

The transformed probability density is

$$f_{WX}(w, x) = |J| f_{\Delta_t \Delta_s}(w, z - w)$$

11-41

where J is the Jacobian of the transformation

$$J = \begin{vmatrix} 1 & 1 \\ 1 & 0 \end{vmatrix} = -1.$$

11-42

We have,

$$f_{WZ}(w, z) = |-1| \frac{1}{2\pi \sigma_t \sigma_s} e^{-\left(\frac{w^2}{2\sigma_t^2} + \frac{(z-w)^2}{2\sigma_s^2}\right)}.$$

11-43

Furthermore, our desired result transforms as

$$f_{\Delta_t | \Delta_t + \Delta_s = S}(\delta_t | \delta_t + \delta_s = S) = f_{W|Z}(w | z = s).$$

11-44

The conditional density is the ratio of the joint density and the marginal density

$$f_{W|Z}(w|z) = \frac{f_{WZ}(w,z)}{f_Z(z)}.$$

11-45

The marginal density is

$$f_Z(z) = \int_{-\infty}^{\infty} f_{WZ}(w, z) dw.$$

11-46

The computation of the marginal density is straightforward (though lengthy) and finds

$$f_Z(z) = \frac{1}{2\pi\sigma_t\sigma_s}\sqrt{\frac{2\pi\sigma_t^2\sigma_s^2}{\sigma_t^2+\sigma_s^2}}\, e^{-\frac{\left(\sigma_t^2-\frac{\sigma_t^4}{\sigma_t^2+\sigma_s^2}\right)z^2}{2\sigma_t^2\sigma_s^2}}.$$

11-47

The conditional density is then

$$f_{W|Z}(w|z) = \frac{1}{\sigma\sqrt{2\pi}}\, e^{-\frac{\left(w-\left(\frac{\sigma}{\sigma_s}\right)^2 z\right)^2}{2\sigma^2}} = N\left(\frac{\sigma^2}{\sigma_s^2}z,\sigma^2\right).$$

11-48

where $\sigma = \frac{\sigma_t\sigma_s}{\sqrt{\sigma_t^2+\sigma_s^2}}$.

In terms of the original parameters, $\sigma_t^2 = \bar{\sigma}^2 t$, $\sigma_s^2 = \bar{\sigma}^2 s$, thus

$$\sigma = \sqrt{\frac{st}{s+t}},$$

11-49

and the density is

$$f_{W|Z}(w|z) = \sqrt{\frac{(s+t)}{2\pi st}}\, e^{-\frac{s+t}{2st}\left(w-\frac{t}{s+t}z\right)^2}$$

$$= N\left(\frac{t}{s+t}z,\frac{st}{s+t}\right)$$

11-50

The desired distribution is a normal distribution, however, the distribution mean is offset in the direction of the known value $z=S$ and the variance is scaled.

In fact, the mean of the distribution is precisely at the point joining the initial and final points along a line.

Additionally, this technique may be used to create a sample Wiener process where the values of the endpoints of the process are predetermined.

The result of the previous example may be extended to any process that has stationary independent increments. Let $f_X(x)$ be the density function of the process. The value of the process after n increments is the partial sum of random variables

$$B_n = \sum_{i=1}^{n} X_i$$

11-51

We wish to interpolate between two consecutive points. First, construct the joint probability density function

$$f_{XY}(x, y) = f_X(x)f_Y(y) \qquad \text{11-52}$$

Transform this with the change of variables

$$Z = X + Y$$
$$W = X \qquad \text{11-53}$$

to obtain the transformed density function

$$f_{WZ}(w, z) = f_X(w)f_Y(z - w) \qquad \text{11-54}$$

The desired distribution is the conditional density

$$f_{W|Z}(w|z) = \frac{f_{WZ}(w, z)}{f_Z(z)} \qquad \text{11-55}$$

or,

$$f_{W|Z}(w|z) = \frac{f_X(w)f_Y(z - w)}{\int_{-\infty}^{\infty} f_X(w)f_Y(z - w)dw} \qquad \text{11-56}$$

The numerator is the transformed product and the denominator is the autoconvolution of the distribution.

12 Rationalization Maturity Model

Organizations desiring to improve their portfolio rationalization capabilities may use the list below to determine how efficient portfolio rationalization is in their environment. This list of levels moves from a state with no portfolio rationalization at all, through a manual rationalization process, to a semi-automated process, and finally to a fully-integrated process.

At the final level, portfolio rationalization achieves a degree of Computational Intelligence by self-adjusting the process according to changing conditions. At this point, the process runs automatically with the Rationalization Manager reviewing the results and making manual adjustments when necessary.

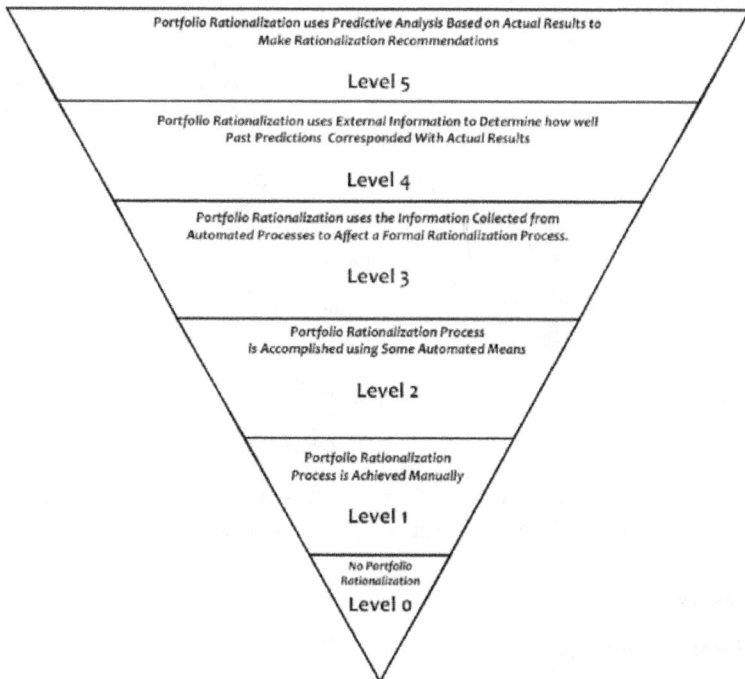

Portfolio Rationalization uses Predictive Analysis Based on Actual Results to Make Rationalization Recommendations

Level 5

Portfolio Rationalization uses External Information to Determine how well Past Predictions Corresponded With Actual Results

Level 4

Portfolio Rationalization uses the Information Collected from Automated Processes to Affect a Formal Rationalization Process.

Level 3

Portfolio Rationalization Process is Accomplished using Some Automated Means

Level 2

Portfolio Rationalization Process is Achieved Manually

Level 1

No Portfolio Rationalization

Level 0

Figure 130: Rationalization Maturity Model Pyramid

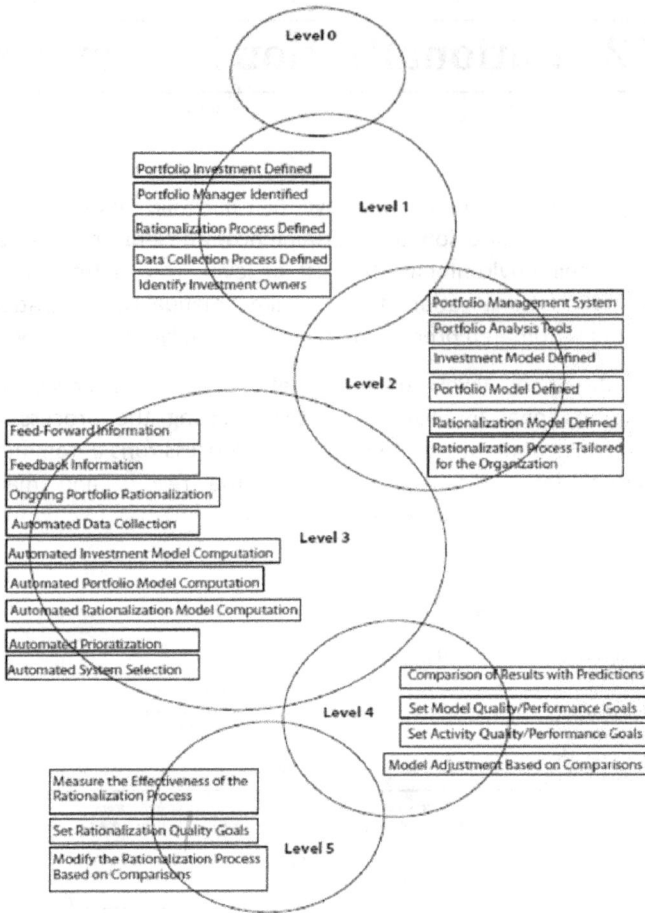

Figure 131: Level decomposition of the Rationalization Maturity Model.

Level 0 – No Portfolio Rationalization Process.

Level 1 – At this level the basic foundation of a Portfolio Rationalization Process is achieved. Portfolio Rationalization is accomplished via manual operations. Executives, directors, and Portfolio Managers typically perform rationalization operations without a formalized process.

The achievements at this level are:

a) ***Portfolio Investments Defined*** – The portfolio is defined in terms of a specific set of investments. Typically, an investment belongs to a single portfolio. Otherwise, different Portfolio Managers may choose to treat the same investment in different ways, leading to conflict between the managers and an unclear direction for the investment.

b) ***Portfolio Manager Identified*** – A Portfolio Manager is identified to manage the portfolio. Instead of a single individual, a committee may be identified to manage the portfolio. In either case, management authority should be clearly laid out and communicated to all stakeholders.

c) ***Rationalization Process Defined*** – A specific Portfolio Rationalization Process should be defined and documented. A well documented process should specify the steps of the rationalization process, what is to be accomplished in each step, who is responsible, who is accountable, who will be consulted, and who is informed.

d) ***Data Collection Process Defined*** – Portfolio Rationalization depends on accurate data for the Portfolio Snapshot. The Portfolio Snapshot is the foundation for the rest of the Portfolio Rationalization Processes. Because the snapshot data is essential to the Portfolio Rationalization Process, it is important to clearly define the data collection process.

e) ***Identify Investment Owners*** – The Portfolio Manager must work with the Investment Owners in order to gather accurate investment information, determine requirements, and identify opportunities for rationalization. It is important to document who the Investment Owners are and who is the primary point of contact for each investment.

Level 2 – Portfolio Rationalization is accomplished using automated means. At this stage, some automated processes are in place to assist with the rationalization process.

a) ***Portfolio Management System*** – The Portfolio Management System is used to collect portfolio information in a central data repository. Investment Owners may independently and continuously update this repository, providing continuous data acquisition to the Portfolio Rationalization Process.

b) ***Portfolio Analysis Tools*** – Portfolio Analysis Tools are used to analyze portfolio data to determine the health of the investments. These tools may be used to assist with any of the Portfolio Rationalization Processes. Tools may be generic such as spreadsheet applications or may be specifically developed for Portfolio Rationalization.

c) *Investment Model Defined* – An Investment Model should be documented for the portfolio. The documentation should specify the activities of the Investment Model, inputs and outputs that are created, and the tools and techniques used.

d) *Portfolio Model Defined* – A Portfolio Model should be documented for the portfolio. The documentation should specify the activities of the Portfolio Model, inputs and outputs that are created, and the tools and techniques used.

e) *Rationalization Model Defined* – A Rationalization Model should be documented for the portfolio. The documentation should specify the activities of the Rationalization Model, inputs and outputs that are created, and the tools and techniques used.

f) *Rationalization Process Tailored for the Organization* – The rationalization process is tailored to the needs of the organization. The documentation for the tailored process should specify the activities of the Portfolio Rationalization Process, inputs and outputs that are created, and the tools and techniques used.

Level 3 – Portfolio Rationalization uses the information collected from automated processes to affect a formal rationalization process. At this stage, the organization has a formalized rationalization process with some automation tools in place to feed information between processes.

a) *Feed-forward Information* – One process feeds a subsequent process. This is the norm for process flows as information is inputted, processed, and then outputted to another process.

b) *Feedback Information* – One process feeds a previous process. Feedback or recurrent information flows are typical. However, feedback information flows are effective for updating the process as new information becomes available. In many cases, it is important in portfolio rationalization to allow new information from one process to update a prior process.

c) *Ongoing Portfolio Rationalization* – Portfolio rationalization should be an ongoing operation, not a year-to-year process. Small, static investment portfolios may not need continuous rationalization. However, many portfolios need continuous monitoring. Without continuous review, rationalization opportunities may be lost and efficiencies unrealized.

d) *Automated Data Collection* – Automating the Portfolio Rationalization Process requires an automated data collection system. This may be accomplished as part of the Portfolio Management System, or through other means. Automated data collection provides regular, continuous data acquisition for the Portfolio Rationalization Process.

e) ***Automated Investment Model Computation*** – The Investment Model is automatically recomputed. Here, the Investment Model is specified to the point where it can be programmatically implemented and computed. The Investment Model may be automatically computed as result of an external trigger (new investment data, process adjustments, etc.) or may be regularly scheduled.

f) ***Automated Portfolio Model Computation*** – This is similar to the Investment Model above, but applied to the Portfolio Model. The Portfolio Model is specified to the degree that it can be programmatically implemented and automatically computed.

g) ***Automated Rationalization Model Computation*** – Similar to the Investment and Portfolio Models above, the Rationalization Model is specified to the point where it may be programmatically implemented and computed automatically based on available data.

h) ***Automated Prioritization*** – The Prioritization process may be automatically completed from available information. Automation of this process automatically identifies potential rationalization targets. The prioritized investments are sent to the Rationalization Manager for consideration.

i) ***Automated System Selection*** – The System Selection process is automated. The Selected Systems are automatically identified and presented to the Rationalization Manager. Automation of this process also identifies systems that may be used to identify Organizational Best Practices.

It is important to distinguish the feedback and feed-forward information flows. A mature organization will likely have portfolio rationalization as a continual process while a less mature organization will perform rationalization sequentially on occasion. When an organization is using feedback information, this is an indicator that the organization has reached a level of maturity where portfolio rationalization is treated as an ongoing operation rather than a one-off project.

Automation of the Portfolio Rationalization Process is a significant achievement. As the process becomes more automated, reliable, consistent results are achieved. This allows Executives to play a larger role in the process as the automation of the results provides them the opportunity to specify the operating parameters of the process without needing to regularly monitor the process activities.

Level 4 – Portfolio Rationalization uses external information to determine how well past predictions corresponded with actual results. Part of the Portfolio Rationalization Process is to make investment and Portfolio Performance predictions. It is important to see how well these predictions matched with reality.

This helps not only to determine how accurate the predictions were, but also to make better predictions in the future. When we have the opportunity of hindsight to see how our predictions compared with reality, we can make adjustments to future predictions to become more accurate.

a) ***Comparison of Results with Predictions*** - The Portfolio Rationalization Process makes predictions of future performance of investments and the portfolio. These predictions can be later matched up against the actual outcomes. By comparing the predictions with the actual results, we can identify potential problems with the models. Recommendations for improvement are provided to the Rationalization Manager.

b) ***Set Model Quality/Performance Goals*** – Overall performance and/or quality goals are set for the Investment Model, Portfolio Model, and the Rationalization Model. The actual results of the models are measured over time and compared with the performance/quality goals. Recommendations for improvement are made and provided to the Rationalization Manager.

c) ***Set Activity Quality/Performance Goals*** – Performance and/or quality goals are specified for each of the model activities. Actual results of the processes are compared to the goals, and recommendations for improvement are provided to the Rationalization Manager.

d) ***Model Adjustment Based on Comparisons*** – The Investment Model, Portfolio Model, or Rationalization Model is adjusted based on results of comparing prior predictions with actual results.

Level 5 – Portfolio Rationalization uses predictive analysis based on actual results to make rationalization recommendations. At this level, the predictions of the portfolio Rationalization Model are not only checked against actual results, but this information is used to modify the Portfolio Rationalization Process itself. New processes may be added and obsolete processes removed. In a sense, the Portfolio Rationalization Process itself undergoes an automatic rationalization.

a) *Measure the Effectiveness of the Rationalization Process* - Actual results are used to make predictive analysis on the rationalization process. The predictions and actual results are compared, and the overall effectiveness of the Rationalization Process is evaluated. Recommendations to improve the Rationalization Process are given to the Rationalization Manager.

b) *Set Rationalization Quality Goals* – Overall performance and/or quality goals are specified for the Portfolio Rationalization Process. Actual results are measured against the goals, and recommendations for improvement are sent to the Rationalization Manager.

c) *Set Process Quality Goals* – Performance and/or quality goals are specified for each Portfolio Rationalization Process. Actual results are measured against the goals and recommendations for improvement and given to the Rationalization Manager.

d) *Modify the Rationalization Process Based on Comparisons–* The Portfolio Rationalization Process is modified by the Rationalization Manager based on the results of the comparisons.

Determining the Rationalization Maturity Level for a given organization/portfolio is done by reviewing the above achievements and determining which are currently met. A particular Portfolio Rationalization Process may meet achievements over a number of levels. We may describe an organization as RMM 3, meaning that all level three achievements are met. Alternatively, we may say that a rationalization process is level 3-4 meaning all of three and parts of four are implemented.

The list of levels and achievements provide a basis for comparing the maturity of the rationalization process between organizations or portfolios. With increasing levels of maturity, we have an increasing degree of process automation and increasing ability to adjust the rationalization process.

Appendix A – Process Definitions

Action Impact
The Action Impact attempts to quantify how a specific investment action may affect the investment value, portfolio value, investment uncertainty, and portfolio uncertainty.

Architecture Analysis
Specific to IT portfolios, this process reviews the structure and design of software, databases, networks, and deployment in IT systems.

Assess Organizational Needs
Uses the Business Strategy, Business Vision, Statutes & Regulations, and Legal Opinions to create a business case for implementing Portfolio Rationalization.

Asset Information Procedure
The Asset Information Procedure process specifies how Asset Information and System Requirements are identified.

Benefit Risk
The Benefit Risk is a measure of uncertainty of the value of the benefit of the investment.

Best Practice Identification
Identifies investments that are performing well and determines the reasons for their good performance.

Business Value Definition
Process specifies the Mathematical Models and Numerical Methods that will be used to quantify the business value of an asset and the associated uncertainty.

Capability Analysis	Examines the capabilities of the portfolio investments and identifies potential rules to identify rationalization targets based on investment capabilities.
Category Analysis	Category Analysis analyzes the available raw data and determines which categories are suitable for used in computing business value.
Category Coverage	Category Coverage determines how many investments have information available for a given Relational Category.
Category Data Requirements	Minimal quality requirements that must be met in order to consider an Investment or Relational Category as having sufficient quality for consideration.
Category Definition	Process of identifying the high-level investment categories. Investments are grouped by category and a particular investment may be placed in more than one category.
Category Identification	Category Identification examines the list of all available categories, determines how the categories relate, normalizes the information, and compiles the information together into a list of Relational Categories.
Category Risk	Computes the uncertainty in the Investment Category values due to uncertainties in the raw data.
Category Valuation	Categorization Valuation is the process of determining the value of each category for every investment.

Cluster Modeling	Cluster modeling groups investments together using their category values or other characteristics that may be used to group the investments.
Compliance Analysis	Compliance Analysis examines how well the portfolio is conforming to expectations.
Cost Analysis	Examines the present and anticipated cost of the portfolio investments.
Cost Risk	The Cost Risk is a measure of uncertainty of the value of the cost of the investment.
Current Maturity	The Current Maturity measured the current maturity state of the asset and incorporates this information into the Investment Model.
Data Analysis	The Data Analysis category is concerned with measuring the quality of the data used to create the Portfolio Snapshot.
Data Cleansing	Identifies and corrects faulty data from the Portfolio Snapshot.
Data Consistency Analysis	Data Consistency Analysis compared two simultaneous measurements of the same data field.

Data Coverage Analysis	Data Coverage Analysis measures the percent of investments that have useful information for a specific data field.
Data Quality Analysis	The Data Quality Analysis subarea is a quantitative quality control process with respect to the Portfolio Snapshot.
Data Stability Analysis	Data Stability Analysis compares successive Portfolio Snapshots taken over time to estimate the extent and variance of the data.
Dilation Mappings	Identifies Relational Category Mappings that are simple scaling and translations of the Investment Categories.
Division Analysis	Analyzes investment requirements, purpose, and function to identify investments that may benefit from dividing them into smaller investments.
Expense Avoidance	Identifies potential cost savings from the portfolio investments. These coast savings may be viewed as a return on the investment.
Feasibility	Feasibility examines the future capability of the investment.
Formulate Performance Expectations	Determines and documents the performance expectations for the portfolio.

Gap Analysis Analyzes investment requirements, purpose, and function to identify gaps.

Gather Asset Information The Gather Asset Information implements all or part of the Asset Information Procedure to obtain a specific set of data.

Governance Measures how the portfolio has performed as compared to the governance expectations of the organization.

Identify Portfolio Investments Specifies the particular investments for a portfolio.

Identify Statutes and Regulations Identify Statutes and Regulations determines how the portfolio is affected by Federal, State, and Local laws.

Identify Strategy & Vision Identify Strategy & Vision identifies the Business Strategy and Business Vision documentation.

Impact Analysis Impact Analysis attempts to quantify the impact the investment has on the overall portfolio, and what impact changes to the investment may have.

Inaction Impact The Inaction Action Impact attempts to quantify how inaction may affect the investment value, portfolio value, investment uncertainty, and portfolio uncertainty.

Investment Division	Reviews requirements, purpose, and functionality of the investments to identify projects, programs, processes, services, products, vendors, or contracts that may be divided over multiple investments.
Investment Gap	Reviews requirements, purpose, and functionality of the investments to identify projects, programs, processes, services, products, vendors, or contracts that may have gaps.
Investment Merger	Reviews requirements, purpose, and functionality of the investments to identify projects, programs, processes, services, products, vendors, or contracts that may be merged.
Investment Model Analysis	Investment Model Analysis identifies potential investment models and selects the particular Investment Model used to compute Business Value.
Investment Model Definition	Investment Model Definition is the determination and specification of a particular model or models to assess the Business Value of an Investment based on the data available.
Investment Obsolescence	Reviews requirements, purpose, and functionality of the investments to identify projects, programs, processes, services, products, vendors, or contracts that may be obsolete.
Investment Phase	Categorizes investments and computes the investment business value.
Investment Redundancy	Reviews requirements, purpose, and functionality of the investments to identify projects, programs, processes, services, products, vendors, or contracts that may be redundant.

Investment Regression Analysis	Regression Analysis is a common technique used to analyze multi-dimensional data sets. Regression Analysis can readily incorporate both values and uncertainties.
Investment Reuse	Reviews requirements, purpose, and functionality of the investments to identify projects, programs, processes, services, products, vendors, or contracts that may be reused.
Investment Risk Analysis	Evaluates risks related to the investments specifically for benefits and costs.
Investment Valuation	Investment Valuation is the process of computing the overall business value(s) for each investment.
Investment Variation Analysis	Variation Analysis is used to compute the uncertainty of the Investment Value.
Linear Mappings	Identifies Relational Category Mappings that are linear combinations of Investment Categories.
Mapping Risk	Computes the uncertainty in the Relational Category value arising from the mapping between the Investment Categories and the Relational Category.
Mappings Analysis	Examines potential mappings between Relational Categories to formulate business value.

Maturity Analysis	Maturity Analysis quantifies an investments level of maturity.
Merger Analysis	Analyzes investment requirements, purpose, and function to identify investments that may be merged.
Monitor & Control	Functions as process improvement, quality control, and quality assurance for the Portfolio Rationalization process.
Nonlinear Mappings	Identifies Relational Category Mappings that are nonlinear in the Investment Category(ies).
Obsolescence Analysis	Analyzes investment requirements, purpose, and function to identify obsolete investments.
Performance Analysis	Examines the contribution of each investment to the overall performance of the portfolio.
Performance Compliance	Measures how the portfolio has performed as compared to prior expectations.
Portfolio Benefits	Examines the benefits that each investment brings to the portfolio.

Portfolio Future Cost	Estimates the present value of the future cost of the investments.
Portfolio Future Maturity	The Future Maturity measured the future maturity state of the asset and incorporates this information into the Investment Model.
Portfolio Model Analysis	Identifies the Portfolio Model used to measure the performance model for the overall portfolio.
Portfolio Model Definition	Identifies the set of values used to quantify portfolio performance.
Portfolio Phase	The Portfolio Analysis phase focuses on analyzing the portfolio as a whole and makes recommendations for investment rationalization.
Portfolio Present Cost	Reviews the present and past cost of the investments.
Portfolio Regression Analysis	Examines the portfolio investment data and creates one or more models to extrapolate the data characteristics.
Portfolio Risk	Quantifies the uncertainties in the portfolio values.

Portfolio Risk Analysis	Examines the uncertainties and sensitivities for the portfolio values.
Portfolio Snapshot	Process of constructing a portfolio snapshot from investment data taken at a particular instant.
Portfolio Valuation	Implements the Portfolio Model and quantifies the performance and uncertainty of the portfolio.
Portfolio Valuation Analysis	Examines the regression models and variations to identify potential values that may be used to measure portfolio performance.
Portfolio Value Definition	Determines the Portfolio Model used to measure the performance and uncertainty of the portfolio.
Portfolio Variation Analysis	Examines how sensitive the regression models are to perturbations in the investment values.
Prioritization	Prioritization is the process of rank ordering the current portfolio assets according to their overall performance, and rank ordering potential new investments.
Program Approval	Formal approval of the implementation of Portfolio Rationalization.

Projected Portfolio Returns	Estimates the present value of potential future returns for the portfolio investments.
Projected System Returns	Estimates the expected future returns for the system of investments.
Rationalization Model Analysis	Identifies a model used to select particular investments for rationalization.
Rationalization Model Definition	Formalizes the rules from Requirements Analysis, Architecture Analysis, Performance Analysis, Compliance Analysis, and Capability Analysis to create a comprehensive set of rules used to identify rationalization targets.
Rationalization Selection	Identifies specific investments targeted for rationalization.
Redundancy Analysis	Analyzes investment requirements, purpose, and function to identify redundant investments.
Regulatory Compliance	Measures how the portfolio has performed as compared to Federal, State, and Local regulations.
Requirements Analysis	Reviews and compiles the requirements, purpose, and functionality of the portfolio investments.

Resource Division	Reviews requirements, purpose, and functionality of resources to identify personnel, equipment, infrastructure, facilities, or licenses that may be used on multiple investments.
Resource Gap	Reviews requirements, purpose, and functionality of resources to identify personnel, equipment, infrastructure, facilities, or licenses that may have gaps.
Resource Merger	Reviews requirements, purpose, and functionality of resources to identify personnel, equipment, infrastructure, facilities, or licenses that may be placed together on an investment.
Resource Obsolescence	Reviews requirements, purpose, and functionality of resources to identify personnel, equipment, infrastructure, facilities, or licenses that may be obsolete.
Resource Redundancy	Reviews requirements, purpose, and functionality of resources to identify personnel, equipment, infrastructure, facilities, or licenses that may be redundant.
Resource Reuse	Reviews requirements, purpose, and functionality of resources to identify personnel, equipment, infrastructure, facilities, or licenses that may be reused.
Return Analysis	Examines the potential returns that the portfolio may receive from the investments.
Reuse Analysis	Analyzes investment requirements, purpose, and function to identify reusable investments.

RMM Level 0   No Portfolio Rationalization.

RMM Level 1   Portfolio Rationalization accomplished via manual operations.

RMM Level 2   Portfolio Rationalization is accomplished using some automated mechanisms.

RMM Level 3   Portfolio Rationalization uses the information collected from automated processes to affect a formal rationalization process.

RMM Level 4   Portfolio Rationalization uses external information to determine how well predictions correspond to actual results.

RMM Level 5   Portfolio Rationalization uses predictive analysis based on actual results to make rationalization recommendations.

Sensitivity   Analyzes how sensitive the portfolio values are with respect to perturbations in their values.

Strategic Alignment   The Strategic Alignment process analyzes the portfolio investments to identify areas that are aligned with the Business Vision and areas that are not.

Strategic Direction	The Strategic Direction process reviews the cluster model, investment prioritization, and investments selected for rationalization to evaluate which investments are performing well and identify problem assets.
System Benefits	Reviews the benefits that each investment brings to the overall system.
System Cost Analysis	Analyzes the present and anticipated future costs of the investments. The costs are used to quantify the return during System Return Analysis.
System Evaluation	Examines the investments selected from the System Selection process and details the investment requirements, purpose, and functionality.
System Expense Avoidance	Quantifies the savings the investments bring to the system.
System Future Cost	Computes the present value of anticipated future costs of an investment.
System Model Analysis	Combines the System Cost Analysis, System Risk Analysis, and System Return Analysis to formulate the System Model.
System Model Definition	Reviews the mathematical models from System Valuation to determine the overall models used to compute the system values.

System Phase	The System Phase examines groups of investments and identifies value that a group of investments has above the value of the constituent investments.
System Present Cost	Examines the current and prior cost of the investments in a system.
System Regression Analysis	Process using statistical techniques to create models from data in a scatter-plot format.
System Return Analysis	Examines the potential returns that the system may incur.
System Risk Analysis	Quantifies the uncertainties in the system values.
System Risk Analysis	Process quantifying the uncertainties in the System Values.
System Selection	The Selection process determines a list of investments The Selection process determines a list of investments for deeper investigation based on the rankings from Prioritization Rationalization.
System Sensitivity	Examines how sensitive the system values are with respect to perturbations in the underlying investment values.

System Valuation Analysis   Identifies potential mathematical expressions for quantifying system value.

System Variation Analysis   Examines the sensitivity and uncertainty in the System Regression Analysis.

Tailor the Process   Tailor the Process identifies the processes and techniques that are implemented in the Portfolio Rationalization process.

Technical Capability   Technical Capability examines the technical aspects of the investment capability.

Transformation Plan   The transformation plan documents specific actions that should be performed to effect the Strategic Direction Document.

Valuation Model Analysis   Determines the Valuation Model based on the information obtained during Valuation Model Analysis.

Valuation Model Definition   Specifies the mathematical model used to compute the values associated with the Investment and Relational Categories.

Valuation Phase   Analysis to determine the methodologies used to value portfolio investments.

Valuation Risk Analysis

Examines the uncertainties in the Relational Categories due to inherent uncertainties in the data as well as uncertainties from the mappings that produce the Relational Categories.

Appendix B – Tools and Techniques

Alignment Models

Mathematical model used to measure and evaluate the alignment of an investment or group of investments with the Strategic Alignment of the organization.

Change Recommendations

Recommendations for modifying a portfolio of investments.

Computational Intelligence

Intelligent computer systems designed to learn and evolve over time specifically designed to adapt to new situations or information.

Corrective Actions

Actions under consideration to correct an identified issue.

Data Analysis

Data Analysis is the process of gathering, modifying, transforming, and/or modeling data in order to better understand the data information.

Data Coverage

Data Coverage is the ratio of the number of instances where a data field contains useful information to the total number of instances of the data field.

Data Repositories

Data Repositories are collections of investment data such as databases, data warehouses, or project archives.

Field Investigations

Field Investigations are onsite inspection of individual investments such as a facilities tour.

Fitness Models

Numerical or mathematical models used to measure an investment's fitness according to a set of pre-defined criteria.

Interviews

Interviews are discussions with investment owners used to collect data for a particular investment.

Issue Identification

Identification of issues relating to investments in a portfolio.

Legal Research

Research on statutes, regulations, cases, and opinions.

Mathematical Models

Mathematical Models are models of a system or investment based in one or more mathematical expressions.

Numerical Methods

Numerical Methods are the application of computers to estimate the value or risk for an investment.

Performance Models

Mathematical models used to measure the performance of a portfolio.

Quad Charts	Quad Charts are two-dimensional graphs divided into four regions. Typically, the regions designate areas of good performance, bad performance, and mixed performance.
Questionnaires	Questionnaires are written questions submitted to investment owners to obtain information about an investment.
Requirements Analysis	Reviewing, understanding, and documenting the requirements for a system.
Requirements Gathering	Eliciting system requirements using interviews, questionnaires, field investigations, user observation, or other information gathering techniques.
Requirements Matrices	Matrices specifying individual requirements on the rows (columns) and systems on the columns (rows) with an indication of which systems implement which requirements.
Risk Analysis	Risk Analysis is the process of identifying and quantifying factors, both positive and negative, which may influence the value of an investment or portfolio.
Risk Models	Mathematical models used to measure the uncertainty in the valuation of an investment or portfolio.
Statistical Techniques	Techniques such as error propagation and stochastic analysis that rely heavily on statistics.

Status Reports   Status Reports are reports detailing the current status of a project or program.

System Diagrams   A diagram for a collection of systems showing how the systems influence each other.

Taxation Issues   Tax Issues considers the tax related consequences of an investment.

Use Case Models   A method of documenting the requirements of a system.

Appendix C – Inputs and Outputs

Action Impact Document	Documents how a specific investment action may affect the investment value, portfolio value, investment uncertainty, and portfolio uncertainty
Architecture Rules	Rationalization rules based on the IT architecture of systems.
Asset Category Coverage	Computes the coverage for both the Investment and Relational Categories.
Asset Category Data	Detailed data for an investment specifying the values for the Investment Categories and Relational Categories for a particular investment.
Asset Information	Asset Information is a collection of data specifying details about a particular investment.
Asset Information Process	The process for obtaining asset information.
Benefit Risk Document	Document detailing the uncertainty in the value of the benefit of the investment.

Best Practices	Practices that are recognized by the industry or organization as effective.
Business Strategy	Document specifying the organization's mission, vision, and objectives and direction for achieving the objectives.
Business Vision	Document specifying the core values, purpose, and goals of the organization.
Capability Rules	Rationalization rules based on the system capabilities.
Category Quality Standard	Document specifying the quality standard for the Relational Categories.
Category Risk Assessment	Specifies the uncertainty associated with each Investment Category.
Compliance Rules	Rationalization rules based on the system compliance.
Cost Risk Document	Document detailing the uncertainty in the value of the cost of the investment.

Current Maturity Document   Document describing the current level of maturity for an investment.

Data Consistency Document   Details the results of the Data Consistency Analysis.

Data Coverage Document   Specifies the data coverage for the fields of interest.

Data Quality Document   Documents the data quality for the investment data.

Data Quality Standard   The specific standard expected for data quality for a particular set of data.

Data Stability Document   Documents how the values of the data fields change over time.

Expense Avoidance   Determines the value of the savings to the portfolio by avoiding some expense.

Feasibility Document   Documents the future capabilities of the investments.

Governance Document	Describes the compliance of the portfolio with the organizational governance procedures.
Inaction Impact Document	Documents how a specific investment inaction may affect the investment value, portfolio value, investment uncertainty, and portfolio uncertainty.
Investment Categories	Investment Categories are data fields or combinations of data fields that are used to identify the characteristics of an investment.
Investment Clusters	Investment Clusters are groupings of investments with similar values.
Investment Division Rules	Rationalization rules based on opportunities for investment division.
Investment Gap Rules	Rationalization rules based on requirements gaps.
Investment Merger Rules	Rationalization rules based on opportunities for investment merger.
Investment Model	The Investment model is a mathematical model used to compute the business value(s) for the investments.

Investment Obsolescence Rules

Rationalization rules based on identification of obsolete investments.

Investment Redundancy Rules

Rationalization rules based on identification of redundant investments.

Investment Regression Document

Details the results of the regression analysis for an investment.

Investment Requirements

Specifies the requirements, purpose, and functionality of an investment.

Investment Reuse Rules

Rationalization rules based on opportunities for reuse.

Investment Values

The values assigned to the investments by applying the Investment Model to the Asset Category Data.

Investment Variation Document

Computes the uncertainty in the value of an investment.

Investments for Rationalization

A list of investments identified as targets for rationalization.

IR Category Maps	Maps that associate which raw categories (from the Investment Categories list) to Relational Categories.
Legal Opinion	A written opinion from a lawyer or qualified legal professional detailing the application of law to a specific situation.
Mapping Risk Assessment	Computes the uncertainty in the Relational Category based on the IR Category Map.
Passed Relational Categories	Relational Categories that are found to meet the Category Quality Standard requirements.
Performance Compliance	Measures how the portfolio has performed with respect to an expected or projected value.
Performance Expectations	Objective measures of future portfolio performance.
Performance Rules	Rationalization rules based on portfolio performance.
Portfolio Benefits	Document examining the benefits that each investment brings to the portfolio.

Portfolio Future Cost Analysis   Determines the expected future cost of the investments.

Portfolio Future Maturity Document   Estimates the future maturity level of an investment.

Portfolio Model   A mathematical model used to measure and evaluate the performance of a portfolio.

Portfolio Performance   A measure of the performance of a portfolio relative to objective criteria.

Portfolio Present Cost Analysis   Determines the present and past cost of the investments.

Portfolio Rationalization Business Case   Business case submitted to executive management specifying the recommendation to implement or not implement a portfolio rationalization process.

Portfolio Rationalization Charter   Formal approval to begin a portfolio rationalization process.

Portfolio Rationalization Process   A specific process tailored to the needs of an organization that implements portfolio rationalization.

Portfolio Regression Analysis	Results of regression analysis applied to the portfolio.
Portfolio Requirements Rules	Rationalization rules based on the requirements, purpose and functionality of the investments in the portfolio.
Portfolio Risk	Documents the uncertainties and sensitivities of the portfolio values.
Portfolio Sensitivity	Examines how sensitive the values and predictions are with respect to perturbations in their values.
Portfolio Snapshot	The portfolio snapshot is a collection of investment data taken at a particular instant.
Portfolio Valuation	The value(s) and risk(s) associated with a portfolio of investments.
Portfolio Variation	Examines sensitivity concerns of the models produced from the Portfolio Regression Analysis.
Prioritized Investments	List of investments in rank order.

Process Performance

Observations of the performance of a particular portfolio rationalization process.

Process Updates

Modifications to a portfolio rationalization process.

Projected Portfolio Returns

Estimates the present value of potential future returns for the portfolio investments.

Projected System Returns

Document estimating the expected future returns for the system.

Rationalization Model

Set of rules used to determine which investments will be rationalized.

Regulatory Compliance

Evaluates how well the portfolio has complied with specific statutes and regulations.

Relational Categories

Categories based on Investment Categories that combine, dissect, or parse Investment Category information to create new Categories.

Resource Division Rules

Rationalization rules based on opportunities for resource division.

Resource Gap Rules	Rationalization rules based on gaps in resources.
Resource Merger Rules	Rationalization rules based on opportunities for resource consolidation.
Resource Obsolescence Rules	Rationalization rules based on identification of obsolete resources.
Resource Redundancy Rules	Rationalization rules based on identification of redundant resources.
Resource Requirements	Requirements related to personnel, equipment, infrastructure, licenses, facilities, or other resources.
Resource Reuse Rules	Rationalization rules based on opportunities for resource reuse.
Selected Systems	Systems selected for detailed evaluation.
Statutes and Regulations	Laws applicable to the portfolio rationalization process.

Strategic Alignments	A measure of an investment or group of investments in relation to the Business Strategy.
Strategic Recommendations	Recommendations to better align investments in a portfolio with the Business Strategy or Business Vision.
System Benefits	The value of the system over and above the sum of the constituent investments.
System Business Value	System Business Value is a Business Value assigned to a system of investments. The System Business Value does not need to be simply the sum of the values of the constituent investments. In fact, the System Business Value may have values for investment categories not present in any of the system investments.
System Evaluations	Detailed evaluations of particular systems or investments.
System Expense Avoidance	Document detailing cost savings arising from the system investments.
System Future Cost	Document providing the present value of anticipated future costs of an investment.

System Model   Mathematical model used to compute the
                            value of a system.

System Present   Document examining the current and prior
Cost   cost of the investments in a system.

System Regression   Document detailing the results of the
Analysis   regression analysis.

System   Raw requirements specifying the technical
Requirements   details for a system.

System Risk   Document specifying the uncertainty in the
                            value of a system.

System Selection   Criteria used to selected systems from the
Criteria   rank ordered prioritization list(s).

System Sensitivity   Document   examining   the   predicted
                            performance   of   the   system   based   on
                            perturbations in the underlying investments.

System Valuation   Document Specifying potential mathematical
Analysis   expressions for quantifying system value.

System Variation Analysis	Document examining the sensitivity and uncertainty in the System Regression Analysis.
Technical Capability Document	Examines the technical aspects of the investment capability.
Transformation Plan	A document detailing what investments should be rationalized, what actions should be taken, and how to proceed enacting the rationalization process.
Valuation Model	Base mathematical model describing the fundamental categories that may contribute to the Investment Model.

Appendix D – Roles

Data Manager — Data Managers are responsible for the acquisition, maintenance, storage, and retrieval of investment information.

Executive — Executives are organizational leaders responsible for the strategic direction of the organization as well as approving project and programs.

Investment Owner — An Investment Owner is a person, such as a project manager, who is responsible for an investment.

Legal Expert — Lawyers and other legal staff that provide legal opinions.

Portfolio Manager — Person responsible for the overall management of the portfolio.

Rationalization Manager — Person responsible for the management of the rationalization process.

Stakeholder — Person who has a vested interest and is affected by the outcome of a system's status.

| **System Expert** | System Experts are individuals who are familiar with the technical details of a system and can provide information as subject matter experts. |

Appendix E – Terms

Army Information Technology Portfolio Management Guidance
Additional guidance for interpretation of the DODI 8115.02 instruction as issued by the Army.

Asset
See Investment.

Autoconvolution
Convolution of a function with itself.

Autocorrelation Function
Correlation of a sequence with itself as a function of varying time intervals.

Backpropagation
Backward propagation of the output result through the layers of an artificial neural network.

Best-fit
The optimal fitting in regression where the distance is a minimum.

Business Value
A quantifiable measure and unit associated with an investment.

Category	A defined characteristic that can be identified with all investments within a portfolio.
Clinger-Cohen Act of 1996	A Congressional mandate instructing the Director of the Office of Management and Budget to promote improvements in the use of information technology by the Federal Government.
Cluster	A grouping of investments based on a similar identified characteristic.
Conditional Expectation	Expectation of a result given conditional information.
Conditional Probability	Probability of a result occurring given conditional information.
Conditional Probability Density	Probability density given conditional information.
Dimension	The physical or logical character of a measurement.
DODI 8115.02	Provides interpretation of the OMB Circular A-130 for information technology portfolio management as issued by the Department of Defense.

Error Propagation	Error analysis technique used to determine the error in a function given the errors in the variables of the function.
Feedback Information	One process feeds another process.
Feed-forward Information	One process feeds a subsequent process.
Financial Portfolio	Investments in stocks, bonds, mutual funds, or other securities.
Fitness	A computed value that reflects the overall asset performance based on all quantifiable valuation factors for an investment.
Investment	An investment is a project, program, portfolio, system or other intangible asset present in a non-financial portfolio. Investments are also called Assets or Systems.
Least-Squares	Technique for fitting a curve to a set of measured data.
Legacy	An outdated or obsolete investment.

Linear Regression   A common regression technique to fit measured data to a straight line.

Measure   The measured value of an investment.

Measured Value   A particular observation of a value at some instant in time.

Monte Carlo Simulation   Computerized simulation of events where the simulation is run multiple times using random variables to generate various initial conditions.

Non-Financial Portfolio   Investments in projects, programs, equipment, or other intangible assets.

Normal Distribution   Used to describe data that is clustered about an average.

OMB Circular A-130   Implements the requirements of the Clinger-Cohen Act of 1996 by providing a specific policy for implementation by the heads of Government agencies as issued by the Director of the Office of Management and Budget.

Portfolio   A collection of investments grouped together to achieve a collective purpose.

Portfolio Governance	Executive rules and regulations for a portfolio.
Portfolio Rationalization	The process of analyzing the assets or investments in a portfolio to determine how the investments should be adjusted to better align the portfolio with the strategy of the organization.
Portfolio Rationalization Lifecycle	A continuous, ongoing operation, not a linear procedure used to implement the Portfolio Rationalization process.
Portfolio Value	A defined quantifiable metric unit that helps to measure the overall performance of a portfolio.
Rationalization Target	Identified investments that, when analyzed individually or according to their clusters, appear to be likely candidates for rationalization.
Regression	A technique used for fitting a set of measured data to a curve.
Return	The return, either financial or non-financial, an investment offers to an organization.
Risk	A measure of uncertainty in a value such as probability, vulnerability, and impact.

ROI   Return on Investment.

Stochastic   A process that incorporates a random
Process   element.

Strategic Value *See Business Value.*

System   *See Investment.*

Unit   Units are the particular scale used in
                     measuring a dimension.

Worst-fit   The fitting in regression where the distance is
                     a maximum.

Bibliography

(2008). *Army Information Technology Portfolio Management Guidance*

Becker. (2003). *Process Management.* Springer.

Bonham. (2005). *IT Project Portfolio Management.* Artech House.

Brzezniak. (2000). *Basic Stochastic Processes.* Springer.

Castrup. (2004). Estimating and Combining Uncertainties. *8th Annual ITEA Instrumentation Workshop* .

(2003). *Department of Defense Instruction 8115.01.*

(2003). *Department of Defense Instruction 8115.02.*

Fabozzi, F., Kolm, P., Pachamanova, D., & Focardi, S. (2007). *Robust Portfolio Optimization and Management.* Wiley.

Focardi, S., & Fabozzi, F. (2004). *The Mathematics of Financial Modeling & Investment Management.* Wiley.

Ghasemzadeh, A. a. (1999). An Integrated Framework for Project portfolio Selection. *International Journal of Project Management* .

Gibson. (2008). *Asset Allocation.* McGraw-Hill.

Grigoriu. (2002). *Stochastic Calculus: Applications in Science and Engineering.* Birkhäuser.

Hsu. (1997). *Probability, Random Variables, & Random Processes.* McGraw-Hill.

Infotmation Technology Reform Act of 1996.

Kaplan. (2005). *Strategic Portfolio Management.* PRTM.

Kuhn. (2006). *The Karush-Kuhn-Tucker Theorem.* CDSEM Uni Mannheim.

Lawton, P., & Jankowski, T. (2009). *Investment Performance Measurement.* Wiley.

National Defense Authorization Act of 1996.

Neate. (2002). *An Introduction to Ito Calculus and Stochastic Differential Equations.*

Office of Management and Budget Circular A-11.

Office of Management and Budget Circular A-130.

Pritchard. (2005). *Risk Management.* ESI International.

Rao. (1995). *C++ Neural Networks and Fuzzy logic.* M & T Books.

Rosenthal. (2008). *A First Look at Rigorous Probability Theory.* World Scientific.

Xu. (2005). Survey of Cluster Modeling Algorithms. *IEEE Transactions on Neural Networks* .

Index

www.ingramcontent.com/pod-product-compliance
Lightning Source LLC
Chambersburg PA
CBHW072307210326
41519CB00057B/3049